Business English

Telephoning
& Socializing

crpdu **Hawoo**

Business English
Telephoning&Socializing

초 판 1쇄 발행 2014년 8월 29일

저자 크레듀 외국어연구소
기획 크레듀 외국어연구소

펴낸이 박민우
기획팀 송인성, 김선명, 박민하
편집팀 박우진, 박영숙, 김영주, 김정아, 최미라
관리팀 임선희, 정철호, 김성언, 라영일
펴낸곳 (주)도서출판 하우
주소 서울시 중랑구 망우로68길 48
전화 (02)922-7090
팩스 (02)922-7092
홈페이지 http://www.hawoo.co.kr
e-mail hawoo@hawoo.co.kr
등록번호 제306-2004-22호

값 20,000원
ISBN 978-89-7699-984-9

Copyright ⓒ 2014 by Credu Co., Ltd.

All rights reserved.
No part of this publication may be reproduced, stored in a retrieval system,
or transmitted in any form or by any means, electronic, mechanical, photocopying, recording,
or otherwise, without the prior permission of the publisher.

이 책은 저작권법에 따라 보호받는 저작물이므로 무단전재와 무단복제를 금지하며,
이 책 내용의 전부 또는 일부를 이용하려면 반드시 (주)크레듀와 (주)도서출판 하우의 서면 동의를 받아야 합니다.

Contents

Part I Telephoning

Chapter 01	**Basics of Telephoning** - Greeting, Purpose	6
Chapter 02	**Information** - Requesting / Verifying Information	16
Chapter 03	**Putting on Hold** - Asking to Wait, Directing a Call	26
Chapter 04	**Message and Note** - Taking a Message, Leaving a Message	36
Chapter 05	**Appointments** - Making Appointments	46
Chapter 06	**Problems** - Dealing with Problems	56
Chapter 07	**Orders** - Sales Related Calls	66
Chapter 08	**Agreement** - Reaching Agreement	76
Chapter 09	**Wrap Up** - Ending a Conversation	86
Chapter 10	**Calling Back** - Keeping Posted	96

Part II Socializing

Chapter 11	**Introduction & Greeting** - Formal Introduction & Getting to Know Someone	108
Chapter 12	**Welcoming** - Receiving Visitors	118
Chapter 13	**Meeting** - Issues and Schedules	128
Chapter 14	**Small Talk** - Talking about Vacations	138
Chapter 15	**Small Talk** - Talking about Health & Lifestyle	148
Chapter 16	**Small Talk** - Talking about Social Networking	158
Chapter 17	**Arrangements** - Getting Together	168
Chapter 18	**Leading Conversation** - Holding/Changing the Topic	178
Chapter 19	**Dining** - Business Meals / Drinks	188
Chapter 20	**Saying Goodbye** - Business Etiquette	198

Part I
Telephoning

Chapter 01: Basics of Telephoning

Greeting, Purpose

In business situations, you could make or receive a call, so you should know how to properly greet and state the purpose of your call. Let's learn the expressions and phrases regarding the basics of telephoning in English.

📷 SNAPSHOT

Let's learn key vocabulary/phrases you would use in introduction and greeting situations.

Hello?	calling	telephone number	message
memo	Good morning.	in order to	This is she/he.
Speaking.	Hold on.		

🔍 TODAY'S SITUATION

Mr. Gauvain calls Mr. Bix's office in order to ask him to present a conference speech. Let's learn the sentence patterns and key expressions.

A: Good morning. I'd like to speak to Gravan Bix, please.

B: Who's calling, please?

A: It's Jean-Pierre Gauvain from Paris.

B: I'm afraid he's talking on another line. Can I take a message?

A: Yes. I called him in order to ask him if he can give a talk at the conference that I am planning.

B: Of course, but probably you should speak to Peter James. He often gives talks at conferences.

A: Peter James? Good. Could you put me through to Peter James instead of leaving a message for Gravan Bix?

B: Sure, just hold for one moment. Bye.

A: Thanks a million. Good- bye.

B: Bye.

✏️ Check Point

- 전화 통화를 시작하는 표현: **Good morning.**
  여보세요?
- 전화 통화 상대방이 누구인지 묻는 표현: **Who's calling, please?**
  당신은 누구 십니까?
- 전화 통화에서 자신을 소개하는 표현: **It's A.**
  저는 A입니다..
- 전화를 건 목적을 나타내는 표현: **I called A in order to B.**
  저는 A에게 B하기 위하여 전화했습니다.
- 전화를 끊을 때 사용하는 표현: **Good-bye. / Bye.**
  안녕히 계세요

💬 Further Expressions

- 전화 통화를 시작하는 표현: 여보세요?
  - Good morning/afternoon/evening.
  - Hello?

- 전화 통화에서 자신을 소개하는 표현: 저는 A입니다.
  - It's A.
  - This is A.
  - I am A.
  - A, speaking.

- 잠시 기다리라는 표현: 잠시만 기다리세요.
  - Wait a minute/moment/second.
  - Hold on, please.
  - Hold on a second, please.
  - Please, hold.

🔍 PATTERN PRACTICE

Practice with a Partner

Let's practice the dialogue patterns and expressions that you have just learned with your partner.

A:

B:

A:

B:

A:

B:

EXTRA EXPRESSIONS

A: I'd like to speak to Gravan Bix, please.
I want to speak to Gravan Bix, please.
Can I speak to Gravan Bix, please?
May I speak to Gravan Bix, please?
Could I speak to Gravan Bix, please?

A: I called him <u>in order to ask</u> him if he can give a talk at the conference that I am planning.
I called him <u>to ask</u> him if he can give a talk at the conference that I am planning.
I called him <u>for asking</u> him if he can give a talk at the conference that I am planning.

🔍 PRACTICE BY YOURSELF

1. Vocabulary Check-up

Match the words with the correct definition.

① give a talk   •   • Ⓐ leave word

② put through   •   • Ⓑ give a lecture about a particular subject

③ leave a message •   • Ⓒ to connect somebody to somebody else by telephone

④ conference   •   • Ⓓ to hold something/somebody tightly; to not let go of something/somebody

⑤ hold on   •   • Ⓔ a meeting, often lasting a few days, which is organized on a particular subject or to bring together people who have a common interest

Complete the sentence with a proper word. Change the form if needed.

① A few years ago, when I was back in school, I _____ at my old college.

② Could you _____ me _____ to the manager, please?

③ I should attend a _____ on education next month.

④ Please, _____ for just a moment.

⑤ If you _____, I'll return your call as soon as possible.

2. Sentence Paraphrasing

> Practice some other sentences out loud keeping the same meaning with the given sentence.

① Hold on, please.

② I'd like to speak to Gravan Bix, please.

③ I called him in order to ask him if he can give a talk at the conference that I am planning.

Telephone Etiquette in Business

1. Things to do to make a nice first impression on the phone:

① Answer promptly (by the third ring).
② Always identify yourself & department.
③ Be polite and courteous.
④ Before picking up the receiver, end any other side conversations and ignore distractions, such as incoming emails.
⑤ Smile! — It shows, even through the phone lines.
⑥ Speak clearly and enunciate.
⑦ Never talk with anything in your mouth - including gum!
⑧ Don't interrupt.
⑨ Seek clarification: "If I understand correctly…"

MAKE MY OWN DIALOGUE

Idea Bank

What is the difference between a business call and a casual call?

Let's compare a business call and a casual call that you had recently.

Business Call	Casual Call
❶ Who did you talk to?	❶ Who did you talk to?
❷ How did you begin the call?	❷ How did you begin the call?
❸ What was the purpose of the call?	❸ What was the purpose of the call?

The big difference between the two types of call is

_____

_____

Class Discussion

When you make or receive a call, you need to identify yourself. What kind of information do you include? If there are more ideas or students come up with other ideas, you can add them to the list.

1. Name
2. Company name
3. Team name

What could be a purpose for calling?

1. To arrange a meeting
2. To request some information
3. To discuss an issue

What gives you bad impression of someone when you're talking on the phone?

1. When someone is distracted
2. When someone puts you on hold without any warning
3. Mumbling, creating noise, grumbling, huffing or sighing, yawning, and being rude
4. Going to the bathroom while using the phone

My Own Dialogue

Choose whether you are a caller or receiver:
_____

Choose a person that you are talking with on the phone:
_____

Choose the purpose of the call:
_____

Based on the above selections, make your own dialogue.

A:

B:

A:

B:

A:

B:

Act Out

Act out your own dialogue in front of the class. You can get help from your partner if you need a dialogue partner.

Teacher's Model Dialogue

Ms. Hathrow from Finance Department calls Mr. Clark in Sales to check some numbers in the sales account.

A: Good afternoon. Thank you for calling ABC Company. This is William Clark. How can I help you?

B: Hello, Mr. Clark. This is Ella Hathrow at Finance Department. How are you doing?

A: I'm very tired nowadays since it's the end of the month, and we have to settle the numbers in sales accounts.

B: Sorry to hear that. The reason I called is to check the numbers that you sent me yesterday. I can't figure out why the ending balance of last year didn't match the beginning balance of this year.

A: I'm sure I double-checked it before sending the documents to you. Let me see. Oh, I see. I made a big mistake. I wrote down the beginning balance of last year as this year. I was out of my mind. I apologize for making such an awful mistake.

B: Oh, no problem. I just wanted to make sure the numbers were correct. Thank you for checking. Well, I better let you go. I don't want to interrupt you anymore.

A: Okay, thank you for calling. Talk to you later. Bye!

Chapter 02 Information

Requesting/Verifying Information

During a business telephone call, you need to know the ways to request or verify information. Let's learn the expressions and phrases regarding information in English.

📷 SNAPSHOT

Let's learn key vocabulary/phrases you would use when requesting or verifying information on the phone.

information	data	true-false	confirmation	100%
I want to know the truth.		verification	double check	asking

🔍 TODAY'S SITUATION

Ms. Briony Rhys is calling in order to request and verify information she needs. Let's learn the sentence patterns and key expressions.

A: Can I have your name, please?

B: Yes, it's Briony Rhys. That's B-R-I-O-N-Y and R-H-Y-S.

A: Oh, yes. We spoke last Thursday, didn't we? Would you like to make a booking?

B:: Well, we're extremely interested, but I want to ask you a few questions before we make our final decision.

A:: OK. Go ahead.

B:: Well, I'm interested in the price of the park tour. Is it still possible to get a discount for a group booking as you said before?

A:: Well, it depends on how many people there will be. If you have more than 20, you can get 20% off.

 Check Point

- 개인정보를 묻는 표현: **Can I have your name, please?**
  성함이 어떻게 되십니까?

- 사실을 확인하는(confirmation) 표현: **We spoke last Thursday, didn't we?**
  우리 지난 목요일에 얘기했죠, 그렇죠?

- 호기심/관심을 나타내는 표현: **I am interested in A.**
  저는 A에 관심이 있습니다.

- 정보를 조회/확인(verifying)하는 표현:
  Is it still possible to A as you said before?
  당신이 지난 번에 말했던 것처럼 A하는 것이 여전히 가능합니까?

Further Expressions

- 개인정보를 묻는 표현:
  - **Can I have your name, please?** 성함이 어떻게 되십니까?
  - **Who's calling, please?** 누구십니까?

- 사실을 확인하는(confirmation) 표현: ~, 그렇죠/맞죠?
  - We spoke last Thursday, didn't we?
  - He doesn't speak any more, does he?
  - You will speak to Jane, won't you?
  - We weren't busy, were we?
  - She is free, isn't she?
  - I will be there, won't I?

- 호기심/관심을 나타내는 표현: 저는 A에 호기심/관심이 있습니다.
  - I am interested in A.
  - I'm interested to know A.
  - I'm so curious about A.
  - I wonder A.

🔍 PATTERN PRACTICE

Practice with a Partner

Let's practice the dialogue patterns and expressions that you have just learned with your partner.

A:

B:

A:

B:

A:

B:

EXTRA EXPRESSIONS

A: Go ahead.
Sure. What is it?
Sure. Continue, please.

B: Is it still <u>possible</u> to get a discount?
Is it still <u>available</u> to get a discount?
<u>Is the opportunity to get a discount still available</u>?

🔍 PRACTICE BY YOURSELF

1. Vocabulary Check-up

Match the words with the correct definition.

① booking •   •Ⓐ You doubt whether something is 100% true or not, so you double check.

② verification •   •Ⓑ You already know the truth and you double check.

③ confirmation •   •Ⓒ the arrangement that you make when you reserve something such as a hotel room, a table at a restaurant, a theatre seat, or a place on public transport

④ curious •   •Ⓓ able to be used or can easily be bought or found

⑤ available •   •Ⓔ interested in something and want to know more about it

Complete the sentence with a proper word. Change the form if needed.

① The data are easy to forge and require secondary _____.

② Jane is _____ a trip to Bali on the Internet.

③ They are _____ about the dove's new eating habits.

④ Please sign below in _____ of the receipt of the package.

⑤ When is his next _____ appointment time?

2. Sentence Paraphrasing

Practice some other sentences out loud keeping the same meaning with the given sentence.

❶ Can I have your name, please?

❷ I am interested in A.

❸ Go ahead.

Telephone Etiquette & Tips in Business

1. ***When giving out information :*** If you answer the phone for work purposes and you need to give out information, such as addresses, web URLs, email addresses, etc., have everything written down and in front of you so that you can spell it out with speed and accuracy and not get tripped up panicking and going blank.

2. ***When talking with native speakers on the phone :*** They usually speak very quickly, and don't pronounce the words well. In that case, you immediately need to ask the person to speak slowly. When taking note of a name or important information, repeat each piece of information as the person speaks. Also, do not say you have understood if you have not. Ask the person to repeat until you have understood.

MAKE MY OWN DIALOGUE

Idea Bank

What is the difference between a business call and a casual call?

Let's compare a business call and personal call to request information that you had lately.

Business Call

❶ Who did you talk to?

❷ What kind of information did you ask for?

❸ Which expressions did you use?

Casual Call

❶ Who did you talk to?

❷ What kind of information did you ask for?

❸ Which expressions did you use?

The big difference between the two types of call is

_____

_____

Class Discussion

In business, you need to request a lot of information to other people. What kind of information do you ask for? If there are more ideas or students come up with other ideas, you can add them to the list.

1. Back data for business reports
2. Traveling information
3. Product information

Which expressions sound polite when requesting something?

1. Could you ~ / Would you ~
2. I would be grateful if you could tell me
3. I need to know (about/if/when/who/how)

If someone gives you information over the phone, what factors could influence understanding right away?

1. Sound level
2. Speaker's speed
3. Speaker's accent

My Own Dialogue

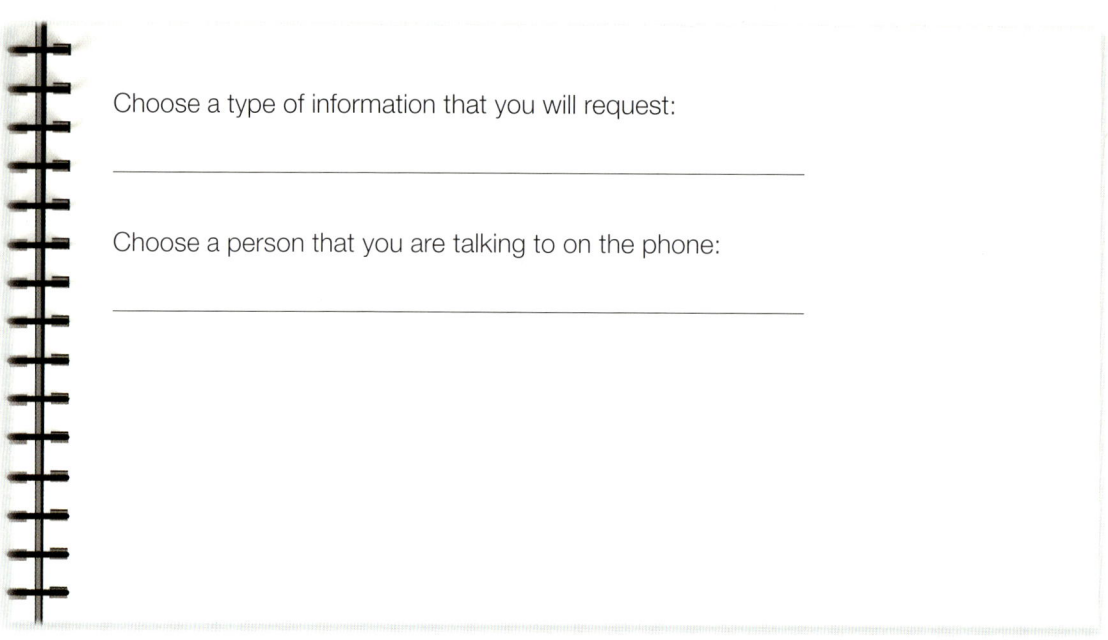

Choose a type of information that you will request:

_____

Choose a person that you are talking to on the phone:

_____

Based on the above selections, make your own dialogue.

A:

B:

A:

B:

A:

B:

Act Out

Act out your own dialogue in front of the class. You can get help from your partner if you need a dialogue partner.

Teacher's Model Dialogue

Ms. Hathrow has a business meeting in New York in 2 weeks, so she calls the travel agency to request information about her trip.

A: Good afternoon. Thank you for calling ABC Travel Agency. This is Sarah Hyland. How can I help you?

B: Hello, Ms. Hyland. This is Ella Hathrow at ABC company. I'm planning to go on a business trip in 2 weeks and would like to get some information about the trip.

A: Oh, Ms. Hathrow. You went to Hong Kong last month, right? What would you like to ask?

B: First, how much is a round-trip flight to New York? Since it's a long flight, I would like to take first class.

A: Well, we need to check the exact date, but first class is running a promotion now, so you can get it if you pay 1.5 times more than the coach price, which makes it $3,500.

B: So you mean the regular price for coach is $2,000 and the prestige one is $3,500, right?

A: You're absolutely right. Do you want to make a reservation?

B: No, not now. I need to fix the schedule with my client. I would also like to know about hotel information and restaurant recommendations.

A: How about sending you those by email? Then you can take time to read through them and make a better decision. I think I still have your email in my database. Let me check. Is your address ellahathrow@abc.com?

B: That's correct. If I don't get an email from you, I'll call you again. Thank you for the help.

Chapter 03
Putting on Hold
Asking someone to wait or directing a call

In a telephone call, you may encounter situations where you need to ask someone to wait or direct a call to somebody. Let's learn the expressions and phrases regarding these situations in English.

📷 SNAPSHOT

Let's learn key vocabulary/phrases you would use when asking someone to wait during a call or directing a call.

Hold on, please.	Wait a minute/moment/second.	transfer
Please.	put through	absent	not available
unavailable	Sorry.	

🔍 TODAY'S SITUATION

Ms. Elaine is on the phone, waiting for Mr. Matti and then asks to direct the call to David. Let's learn the sentence patterns and key expressions.

A: Hello? This is Elaine. I'd like to speak to Matti, please.

B: I'm sorry, but he's talking on another line. Could you wait a minute, please?

A: Sure. Is he busy these days? It is hard to get in touch with him.

B: Since last month, our team has started a new project. It requires lots of energy and effort.

A: Oh, I see. Could you put me through to David? I think it's better to talk to David rather than Matti. Matti seems too busy to talk to me.

B: OK, I will transfer you to David. Hold on, please.

✏️ Check Point

- 전화 통화를 바로 할 수 없음을 나타내는 표현:
  I'm sorry but A is talking on another line. 죄송하지만 A는 다른 전화통화 중입니다.

- 잠시 기다리라는 표현: **Could you wait a minute, please? / Hold on, please.**
  잠시 기다려 주시겠어요?   잠시 기다리세요.

- 전화 통화를 다른 사람에게 연결해 달라는 표현: **Could you put me through to A?**
  A에게 전화를 연결해 주시겠어요?

- 전화 통화를 다른 사람에게 연결해 주겠다는 표현: **I will transfer you to A**
  A에게 전화를 연결해 드리겠습니다.

💬 Further Expressions

- 전화 통화를 바로 할 수 없음을 나타내는 표현:
  - **I'm sorry but A is talking on another line.** 죄송하지만 A는 다른 전화통화 중입니다.
  - **I'm afraid A is not at his/her desk right now.** 죄송하지만 A는 지금 자리에 없습니다.
  - **Sorry, but A must be at lunch.** 죄송합니다만, A씨가 점심식사 중인 것 같습니다.
  - **I'm afraid A is in a meeting.** 죄송하지만 A씨는 지금 회의 중입니다.

- 잠시 기다리라는 표현: 잠시 기다려 주시겠어요? / 잠시만 기다리세요.
  - Could you wait a minute, please?
  - Wait a minute/moment/second.
  - Hold on, please.
  - Hold on a second, please.
  - Please, hold.

- 전화 통화를 다른 사람에게 연결해 주겠다는 표현: A에게 전화를 연결해 드리겠습니다.
  - I will transfer you to A.
  - I will put you through to A.
  - I will connect you to A.

🔍 PATTERN PRACTICE

Practice with a Partner

Let's practice the dialogue patterns and expressions that you have just learned with your partner.

A:

B:

A:

B:

A:

B:

EXTRA EXPRESSIONS

A: Is he busy <u>these days</u>?
Is he busy <u>recently</u>?
Is he busy <u>lately</u>?

B: <u>Since last month</u>, our team <u>has started</u> a new project.
<u>Since 1992</u>, I <u>have changed</u> my goal.
<u>Since they broke up</u>, Sam and Emily <u>have never talked</u>.

🔍 PRACTICE BY YOURSELF

1. Vocabulary Check-up

Match the words with the correct definition.

① transfer   •   • Ⓐ to need something

② require   •   • Ⓑ to connect somebody to somebody else by telephone

③ rather than   •   • Ⓒ to separate or cause to separate

④ break up   •   • Ⓓ instead of

⑤ recent   •   • Ⓔ having happened or started only a short time ago

Complete the sentence with a proper word. Change the form if needed.

① Could you _____ me to Sam, please?

② That's the limit. I'm going to _____ with David.

③ Anne's broken leg will probably _____ surgery.

④ I went to a bookstore to buy John Irving's most _____ book.

⑤ Campbell is intelligent _____ irrational.

2. Sentence Paraphrasing

Practice some other sentences out loud keeping the same meaning with the given sentence.

① Could you wait a minute, please?

② I will put you through to A.

③ Is he busy these days?

Telephoning Etiquette & Tips in Business

1. ***Proper Hold Procedures :*** When talking on the telephone, it is often necessary to place a customer on hold. You may need to place a customer on hold so you can contact another department or transfer the call. Many customers hate being placed on hold, especially if there was a long hold time getting to you in the first place. Before placing the customer on hold, ask for permission. For instance, "Mr. Jones, do you mind if I place you on hold?" If you place the customer on hold, make it brief, no longer than two minutes. If the hold is longer than two minutes, refresh the customer's memory as to what's going on.

2. ***Proper Transfer Procedures:*** Tell the caller the reason you are transferring the call before you do so. Then ask if it is all right to transfer the call. Call the department or person where you are transferring the call to and make sure that they can take the call. If they are able to take the call, give the person's name, the request, any other relevant information. Then return to your caller and give him/her the name of the person he/she is being transferred to, the department, and the telephone number. When you're not sure to whom a call should be transferred, take the caller's name and number, and find out where the call needs to be directed to. Also, give them your name and number as a reference in case the appropriate party does not contact them.

 # MAKE MY OWN DIALOGUE

Idea Bank

How do you handle a call that you received for somebody else?

1. In what kinds of occasions do you receive a call for someone else?

- When my colleague is on the other line
- When my colleague is in a meeting
- When my colleague is taking a leave

2. If the caller says that it's an urgent call, but your colleague is not in his seat at that moment. What would you do?

- Get the caller's contact information
- Try to contact the colleague in a timely manner
- Try to handle the problem on my own or try to figure out solutions

Class Discussion

When making a business call, sometimes you need to wait to talk to someone or your call can be transferred to someone else. What are the things that make you feel bad? If there are more ideas or students come up with other ideas, you can add them up to the list.

1. When I need to wait too long (how long can you wait? why?)
2. When the receiver does not know whom I should talk to
3. When the call keeps going on to transfers (When many transfers occur)

_____

What could be the best way not to make the caller feel bad about the above situations?

1. Tell the caller to call back immediately
2. Figure out to whom the call should be directed
3. Let the caller know the contact information of the person in charge

_____

My Own Dialogue

Choose whether the caller needs to wait or the call should be transferred:

_____

Choose the reason why the intended receiver can't answer the call:

_____

Based on the above selections, make your own dialogue.

A:

B:

A:

B:

A:

B:

Act Out

Act out your own dialogue in front of the class. You can get help from your partner if you need a dialogue partner.

Teacher's Model Dialogue

Ms. Hathrow gets a call for Mr. Clark asking about the sales meeting.

A: Good afternoon. Thank you for calling ABC Company. This is Ella Hathrow. How can I help you?

B: This is Larry Smith at S&E company. I'd like to talk to William Clark, please.

A: Willam Clark from which department?

B: Could you put me through to Mr. Clark in the Sales department?

A: Please hold while I transfer your call …. I'm sorry. I'm afraid Mr. Clark is out of the office at the moment. Could you tell me what it's regarding?

B: Yes, I wanted to check to make sure the sales meeting will be held this Friday as scheduled. He mentioned at the last meeting there might be some changes.

A: Well, Mr. Smith is also in charge of the sales meeting. I think you can discuss the matter with him too. Let me see if he is available. All right. I'll direct your call to Mr. Smith. Just in case, if the call gets cut off, you can call him directly at extension #432. One moment, please.

B: Thank you.

Chapter 04

Messages and Notes

Taking a Message, Leaving a Message

During a business telephone call, you may have to take or leave a message for/to your business partners. Let's learn some expressions and phrases regarding taking or leaving telephone messages in English.

📷 SNAPSHOT

Let's learn key vocabulary/phrases you would use when taking or leaving a telephone message.

message	urgent	accurate memo
concise note	absent colleague	deliver the message
polite to the caller/receiver	confirmation	

_____   _____

_____   _____

🔎 TODAY'S SITUATION

Mr. Aaron McCabe calls Mr. Lars Eller and leaves a telephone message and a voice message. Let's learn the sentence patterns and key expressions.

A: Hello? Could I speak to Mr. Eller, please?

B: I'm afraid he's in a meeting right now. Can I take a message? Who's calling, please?

A: Yes, please. This is Aaron McCabe from Head Office. Can you tell him that the meeting on Friday in Brussels has been cancelled?

B: Aaron McCabe from Head Office called to inform that the Brussels meeting on Friday has been cancelled. Is that right?

A: Perfect. Can you ask him to call me back as soon as possible?

B: No problem. Can you give me your contact number?

A: Yes, it's 01 5487 29445.

<Voicemail message>

A: Hello, Mr. Eller. This is Erin McCabe from Head Office. I called and left a message that the Brussels meeting on Friday has been cancelled. I want to confirm that you've got the message. Please, call me back. My number is 01 5487 29445. Bye.

✎ Check Point

- 메시지를 남기겠는지 묻는 표현: **Can I take a message?** 메시지 남기시겠어요?
- 전화 통화 상대방이 누구인지 묻는 표현: **Who's calling, please?** 당신은 누구 십니까?
- 전화 통화에서 자신을 소개하는 표현: **It's A from B.** 저는 B 소속의 A입니다
- 정보가 맞는지 확인하는 표현: **Is that right?** 맞죠?
- 연락 가능한 전화번호를 묻는 표현: **Can you give me your contact number?** 연락 가능한 전호번호 알려주시겠어요?
- 전화음성 메시지 남기는 형식: **Hello? ~ (MESSAGE) ~ Bye.** 여보세요? ~ (용건) ~ 안녕히 계세요.

💬 Further Expressions

- 메시지를 남기겠는지 묻는 표현: 메시지 남기시겠어요?
  - Can I take a message?
  - May I take your message?
  - Shall I leave him/her a message?
  - Will you leave a message?

- 정보가 맞는지 확인하는 표현: 맞죠?
  - Is that right?
  - Is it okay?
  - Am I right?

- 연락처를 묻는 표현
  - Can you give me your contact number? 연락 가능한 전호번호 알려주시겠어요?
  - Would you mind letting me know your mobile number? 휴대폰 번호를 알려주시겠어요?
  - What is your email address? 이메일 주소가 어떻게 되세요?
  - Please, tell me your extension number. 내선번호 알려주세요.

🔎 PATTERN PRACTICE

Practice with a Partner

Let's practice the dialogue patterns and expressions that you have just learned with your partner.

A:

B:

A:

B:

A:

B:

A:

<Voicemail message>

A:

EXTRA EXPRESSIONS

A: <u>This is</u> Aaron McCabe <u>from Head Office</u>.
<u>It is</u> Aaron McCabe <u>from A&C company</u>.
<u>I am</u> Aaron McCabe <u>from Seoul</u>.

B: No problem.
Sure.
Yes, certainly.
Of course.
Why not?
OK.

🔍 PRACTICE BY YOURSELF

1. Vocabulary Check-up

Match the words with the correct definition.

1. cancel • • Ⓐ to officially tell someone about something or give them information

2. inform • • Ⓑ to telephone somebody again or to telephone somebody who telephoned you earlier

3. call back • • Ⓒ to say that an event that was planned will not happen

4. extension • • Ⓓ one of many telephone lines connected to a central system in a large building, which all have different numbers

5. mobile • • Ⓔ a telephone that you can carry with you and use to make or receive calls wherever you are

Complete the sentence with a proper word. Change the form if needed.

1. Do you know Mr. Brown's _____ number in his company?

2. I'm afraid I'll have to _____ our meeting tomorrow.

3. Please _____ in an hour. Anne will be here then.

4. Please _____ us of any change of address or personal information as soon as possible.

5. Paul Potts was a _____ phone salesman before he became a singer.

2. Sentence Paraphrasing

> Practice some other sentences out loud keeping the same meaning with the given sentence.

❶ Can I take a message?

❷ Is that right?

❸ No problem

Telephoning Etiquette & Tips in Business

1. **When leaving messages:** You need to speak clearly and slowly. Do not use broken phrases, slang, or idioms. Always, leave your return telephone number as part of your message, including the area code. You need to repeat your telephone number at the end of your message. Practice leaving your number, by saying it aloud to yourself as slow as you have heard an informational operator say it.

2. **When leaving a voice-mail message :** No one wants to listen to a lengthy message. Try to make your message short with the following information. Tell your name, company, and your phone number. If your time zone is different, you should mention the date and time. Provide a quick summary of why you're calling. Let them know when you are or aren't available for a callback. One more thing to keep in mind is that in North America leaving a voicemail is ubiquitous and not returning calls left on a personal voicemail system is considered rude.

3. **Preparation for taking messages :** Always be ready to take messages at any time in business. Have pens, pencils, and notepaper nearby your phone, so you can reach them easily.

MAKE MY OWN DIALOGUE

Idea Bank

How do you leave/take messages on the phone?

1. Have you ever left a voice mail or a message on an answering machine?

- Why did you have to leave the voice mail?
  · When the receiver is out of the office for business trips/vacation

  _____

- What information was there in the voice mail greeting?
  · name, the reason for not getting the call, _____
- Where did you leave the message?
  · on the cell phone / the company voice mail
- How did you feel about leaving a message on an answering machine?
  · feels weird talking by oneself, _____
- What information did you leave on that message?
  · name, company, the reason for calling, _____

2. Have you ever taken a message for someone else?

- Why did you take the message?
  · When the colleague was out of the office

  _____

- Where did you write down the message?
  · on a message notepad, a post-it,
- What information did you write on that message?
  · name, company, the reason for calling,
- How did you give the message to the person?
  · left it on the colleague's desk, transferred the message through email, intranet gave the message to him directly,

Class Discussion

On what kind of occasions do you leave a message on the phone? If there are more ideas or students come up with other ideas, you can add them to the list.

1. When the secretary gets a call and says the person that you want to talk is not available
2. When the receiver is on another line or out of the office
3. When you do not know the person's direct number, and the person is busy at the moment
4. When the receiver cannot be reached on his/her cell phone as well

---

In Korea, it's unusual to leave a voicemail message, but in North America, it is common to do so. Let's think back to the times when we used pagers. At that time, we used to have voicemail greetings. What did you use to make a perfect voicemail greeting?

1. Select nice background music
2. Create a script before recording
3. Remove any noise sources from the room you are recording in
4. Preview the recording before saving it

My Own Dialogue

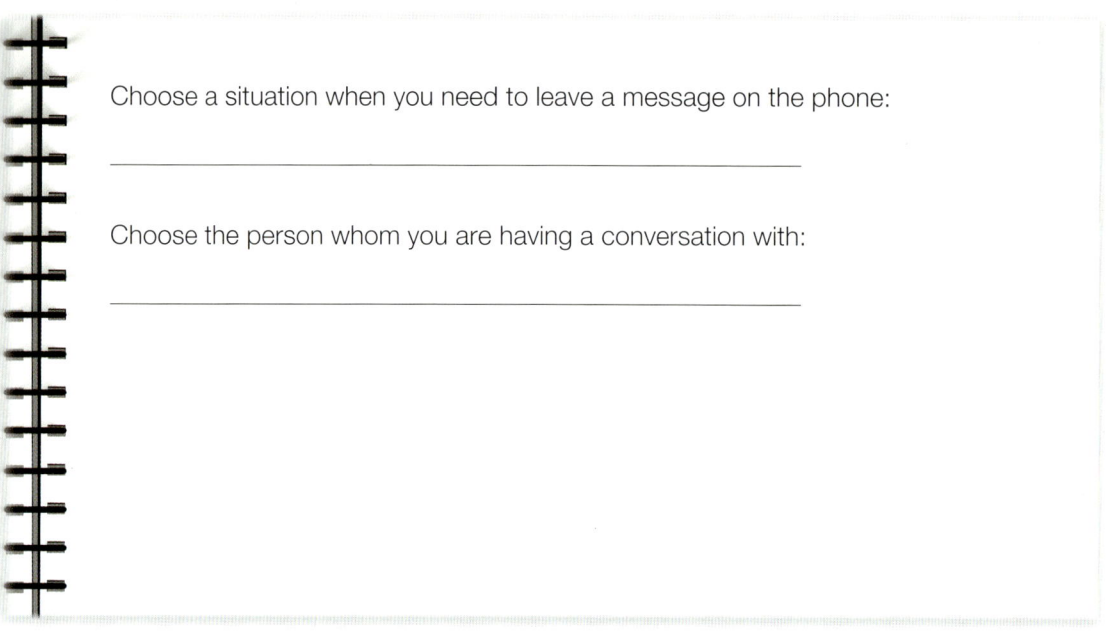

Choose a situation when you need to leave a message on the phone:

_____

Choose the person whom you are having a conversation with:

_____

📝 **Based on the above selections, make your own dialogue.**

A:

B:

A:

B:

A:

B:

Act Out

Act out your own dialogue in front of the class. You can get help from your partner if you need a dialogue partner.

Teacher's Model Dialogue

Ms. Hathrow gets a call for Mr. Clark after he has left for the day.

A: Good afternoon. Thank you for calling ABC Company. This is Ella Hathrow. How can I help you?

B: This is Larry Smith at S&E company. I'd like to talk to William Clark, please.

A: I'm afraid he's gone for the day. He won't be back until tomorrow morning. Would you like to leave a message?

B: Yes, please tell him that I called and would like him to call me back. Oh, please tell him that I cannot be reached by my cell phone since it's broken. I will be at my office, so he should call me at extension number 123.

A: I'd better write this down. Hold on a moment while I find a pen. OK. Go ahead.

B: My office number is 343-3423 and extension is 123.

A: I see. Can I get your name again, please?

B: Larry Smith from S&E company

A: Let me repeat that back to make sure I got it. You're Larry Smith at S&E, and the contact number is 343-3423, extension 123.

B: That's right. Thank you very much.

A: I'll make sure he gets the message.

Chapter 05 Appointments

Making Appointments

In business situations, you need to know how to make and confirm appointments on the phone. Let's learn some expressions and phrases regarding appointments on the phone in English.

📷 SNAPSHOT

Let's learn key vocabulary/phrases you would use when making and confirming appointments on the phone.

make a reservation	booking	travel agency	flight tickets
accommodation	Incheon Airport	business meeting	documents
_____		_____	
_____		_____	

🔍 TODAY'S SITUATION

Mike calls a travel agency in order to make travel arrangements. Let's learn the sentence patterns and key expressions.

A: Four Seasons Travel. Lucy, speaking.

B: Hello, Lucy. This is Mike from DSL Design. I want to make some travel arrangements. I need to book a flight to Boston, USA.

A: OK. Is it a business trip? When will you leave?

B: Yes, I've got an all-day meeting in Boston on the 27th. Can you get me a flight to Boston on the 25th and the return flight on the evening of the 27th or on the 28th?

A: ... to Boston on the 25th, return flight 27th p.m. or the 28th... Do you have any preferences in airline?

B: Yes, the cheapest.

A: I'll put you on the waiting list and see. There is no option right now. I'll call you back as soon as I can find a seat.

B: OK, thanks. Bye.

✎ Check Point

> - 여행 예약을 하는 표현: **I want to make some travel arrangements.**
>   여행 준비를 하고 싶습니다.
>
> - 비행기 티켓을 요구하는 표현: **I need to book a flight to A.**
>   A로 가는 비행기표가 필요합니다.
>
> - 특정 도착지와 시간의 비행기 표를 예약하는 표현:
>   **Can you get me a flight to A on B and the return flight on C?**
>   A지역으로 B날에 출발하는 비행기와 (A지역에서) C날에 돌아오는 비행기표를 주시겠어요?
>
> - 선호하는 것을 묻는 표현: **Do you have any preferences in A?**
>   A 분야에서 선호하는 것이 있으세요?
>
> - 대기자 목록에 올리겠다는 표현: **I'll put you on the waiting list and see.**
>   대기자 목록에 올리고 지켜보겠습니다.

💬 Further Expressions

- 여행 예약을 하는 표현: 여행 준비를 하고 싶습니다.
  - I want to make some travel arrangements.
  - Can I make some travel arrangements?
  - Could I make a reservation for travel?

- 특정 도착지와 시간의 비행기 표를 예약하는 표현:
  A지역으로 B날에 출발하는 비행기와 (A지역에서) C날에 돌아오는 비행기표를 주시겠어요?
  - Can you get me a flight to A on B and the return flight on C?
  - I need a flight ticket to A on B and a return flight on C.
  - Can I make a reservation for a flight to A on B and the return flight on C?

🔍 PATTERN PRACTICE

Practice with a Partner

Let's practice the dialogue patterns and expressions that you have just learned with your partner.

A:

B:

A:

B:

A:

B:

A:

B:

EXTRA EXPRESSIONS

A: Is it a business trip?
Is it travel for vacation/honeymoon/package tour/recreational travel/camping?
Are you going to go on a business trip?

A: I'll call you back in a while.
I'll call you back soon/later/shortly/before long.
I'll call again in a while.
I'll get back to you later.

PRACTICE BY YOURSELF

1. Vocabulary Check-up

Match the words with the correct definition.

1. arrangements • • **A** you like it more than another thing and will choose it if you can

2. accommodation • • **B** plans and preparations that you must make so that something can happen

3. business trip • • **C** travel done in the course of business or work

4. preference • • **D** a place for someone to stay, live, or work

5. waiting list • • **E** a list of people who have asked for something but who must wait before they can have it

Complete each sentence with the proper word. Change the form if needed.

1. Special _____ can be made for guests with disabilities.

2. A _____ could be kind of a bonus to employees.

3. Do you have any color _____ ?

4. Universities have to provide student _____ for freshmen.

5. I was then put on a _____ to see a specialist at the local hospital.

2. Sentence Paraphrasing

Practice some other sentences out loud keeping the same meaning with the given sentence.

① I want to make traveling arrangements.

② Can you get me a flight to A on B and the return flight on C?

③ I'll call you back in a while.

Telephoning Etiquette & Tips in Business

1. **Language difference :** In the UK, "diary" is used for the word "calendar" in the USA. Also, "Bus timetable" is used in the UK, while "Bus schedule" for the USA. For project planning, we use "schedule" or "planner" in both British and US English.

2. **Planning your appointments:** Before planning your appointments, look at your calendar and check for any conflicts. Most professionals know that conflicts may arise at the last minute, and they'll do their best to reschedule you at a more convenient time. Call, apologize for the inconvenience, and choose another time that works for both of you. If you are unsure of a specific time, don't book an appointment then because you don't want to be known as a chronic schedule changer.

3. **Rescheduling:** When you must reschedule, give the other person the opportunity to let you know when he or she is available. Don't go on and on about how busy you are. That doesn't fly since the other person is probably just as busy. Always call to reschedule rather than relying on texts or email. The back and forth conversation can save time and hard feelings. State your name, ask if this is a good time to discuss rescheduling, and simply say that you can't make the appointment. This isn't a time for lame excuses.

MAKE MY OWN DIALOGUE

Idea Bank

What is the difference between making a business appointment and a personal appointment?

Let's compare a business call and a personal call to make an appointment that you had lately.

Business Call	Casual Call
❶ Who did you talk to?	❶ Who did you talk to?
❷ What kind of appointment did you make?	❷ What kind of appointment did you make?
❸ Where and when did you decide to meet?	❸ Where and when did you decide to meet?
❹ How did you get to the agreement on a time?	❹ How did you get to the agreement on a time?

The big difference between the two types of call is

_____

_____

Class Discussion

For what kind of occasions do you need to make appointments on the phone? If there are more ideas or students come up with other ideas, you can add them to the list.

1. When you need to schedule a meeting
2. When you want to have a meal together

What kind of reasons are there for rescheduling or canceling a meeting? Which ones do you consider acceptable or not? Why do you think so?

1. The person who will be at the meeting is sick
2. There is an urgent business issue going on
3. There is a personal issue going on

When making an appointment, what kind of things should be confirmed before ending a call?

1. Place
2. Time
3. People who will be meeting

My Own Dialogue

Choose a person whom you will make an appointment with:
_____

Choose a reason why you need to make an appointment:
_____

Choose a place/time that you will be meeting the person:
_____

Based on the above selections, make your own dialogue.

A:

B:

A:

B:

A:

B:

Act Out

Act out your own dialogue in front of the class. You can get help from your partner if you need a dialogue partner.

Teacher's Model Dialogue

Ms. Hathrow is talking on the phone with Ms. Hyland to make an appointment.

A: Ms. Hyland, when would you like to schedule our meeting?

B: When would be good for you?

B: I'm available on Friday afternoon. Is that convenient for you?

A: Let me check my planner. I'm afraid I have a staff meeting. Could we make it Friday morning instead?

B: Okay, Friday morning is fine. What time? Shall we say 10:30?

A: 10:30 is ideal for me. Where shall we have the meeting? Your office or mine?

B: Oh, our office has a renovated cafe in the lobby, and it has a variety of coffee. I would like to buy you a cup of coffee and then come up to our office to have a meeting. Does that sound fine?

A: I am looking forward to our meeting. I'll see you on Friday at 10:30 at your lobby cafe.

B: Great! See you then.

Chapter 06 Problems

Dealing with Problems

During business calls, you may encounter situations where you have to deal with a variety of problems. Let's learn some expressions and phrases regarding handling problems in English.

📷 SNAPSHOT

Let's learn key of vocabulary/phrases you would use in dealing with problem situations.

apologize	accept	deny	sincere
I'm sorry	fault	misunderstanding	angry
empathize	resolve the problem		

🔍 TODAY'S SITUATION

Mr. Tony Kim makes a call to Kang Taxis and complains about a delay. Let's learn the sentence patterns and key expressions.

A: Kang Taxis. Can I help you?

B: Good afternoon. Yes, I have a problem. I phoned for a taxi for four o'clock, and it still hasn't arrived, and it's now twenty past. This is the longest I've ever had to wait!

A: Oh, that's terrible. I'm sorry about that, sir. Could I have your name, please?

B: It's Tony, Tony Kim.

A: Just a moment, Mr. Tony Kim. Your taxi is on the way. There is road work on the Olympic highway, and the driver says he's never seen such a bad traffic jam on that road. But he'll be there in five minutes. Please accept my apologies. You know this is not a typical situation.

B: Great. Thanks for that. It's not your fault. I'll be waiting outside the house. Bye.

Check Point

- 문제가 발생했음을 나타내는 표현: **I have a problem.**
  저에게 문제가 발생했습니다.

- 나쁜 상황에 대해 공감을 나타내는 표현: **That's terrible.**
  그것 참 끔찍하군요.

- 사과를 나타내는 표현: **I'm sorry about that, sir. /Please accept my apologies.**
  죄송합니다. / 제 사과를 받아주세요.

- 예외적인 상황임을 나타내는 표현: **You know this is not a typical situation.**
  아시다시피 이 상황이 일반적인 상황이 아닙니다

Further Expressions

- 문제가 발생했음을 나타내는 표현: 저에게 문제가 발생했습니다.
  - I have a problem.
  - I've got a problem.
  - I need your help.

- 나쁜 상황에 대해 공감을 나타내는 표현: 그것 참 끔찍하군요.
  - That's terrible/awful/dreadful.
  - I appreciate your situation.
  - I totally understand your terrible situation.

- 사과를 나타내는 표현: 죄송합니다. 제 사과를 받아주세요.
  - I'm sorry about that.
  - Please accept my apologies.
  - Forgive me for that, please.
  - I apologize to you for that.

🔍 PATTERN PRACTICE

Practice with a Partner

Let's practice the dialogue patterns and expressions that you have just learned with your partner.

A:

B:

A:

B:

A:

B:

EXTRA EXPRESSIONS

B: This is the longest I've ever had to wait!
This is the worst (that) I've ever had.
This is the longest that I've ever waited.
I've never waited as long as this.

A: You know this is not a typical situation.
You know this is an unusual/rare/uncommon/infrequent/unfamiliar situation.

PRACTICE BY YOURSELF

1. Vocabulary Check-up

Match the words with the correct definition.

① phone   Ⓐ in the course of journey

② on the way   Ⓑ to speak to someone by telephone

③ road work   Ⓒ something that you say or write to show that you are sorry for doing something wrong

④ traffic jam   Ⓓ repairs or other work being done on a road

⑤ apology   Ⓔ a long line of vehicles on a road that cannot move or can only move very slowly

Complete the sentence with a proper word. Change the form if needed.

① The _____ is making progress steadily with the help of many workers.

② Why didn't they immediately _____ the police?

③ If Anne phones again, tell her I'm _____.

④ Sarah had to make a formal public _____ for her remarks.

⑤ We were stuck in a _____ for two hours.

2. Sentence Paraphrasing

> Practice some other sentences out loud keeping the same meaning with the given sentence.

① I have a problem.

② I'm sorry about that.

③ This is the longest I've ever had to wait!

Telephoning Etiquette & Tips in Business

1. *When you get a complaint call:* First, empathize with the caller. Try to understand how the person is feeling. Apologize and acknowledge the problem. You don't have to agree with the caller but express regret that there is a problem. Accept responsibility. Make sure something is done. Take it upon yourself to do something. Many times they want reassurance that something will be done. They want to know that you care. Use the following phrases, "What can I do for you?" and "I will make sure this message gets to the right person."

2. *Avoid using negative sentences:* Never say the words, "I don't know" when talking with someone on the phone. The ideal response to a question where there is not a definite answer is to say, "I'll check on that for you" or "That is a good question; let me find out for you" or offer to connect the caller with someone who could provide the answer. If a call involves some research, assure the person that you will call back by a specific time. If you do not have an answer by the deadline, call back to say, "I don't have the answer yet, but I'm still working on it". There is no excuse for not returning calls. Also instead of using, "I/we can't do that", say "This is what I/we can do". And instead of "You'll have to", it's better to use "You will need to" or "I need you to" or "Here's how we can help you."

MAKE MY OWN DIALOGUE

Idea Bank

How did you make a complaint and how did you handle a complaint?

Let's think about a complaint that you made and one that you resolved.

The complaint that I made	The complaint that I resolved
❶ When was it?	❶ When was it?
❷ Why did you make the complaint?	❷ Why did you get the complaint?
❸ How did the person you called manage your complaint?	❸ How did you handle it?
❹ Were you happy about the resolution? Why or why not?	❹ Was the caller happy about the resolution? Why or why not?

What did you learn from the two above cases?

_____

_____

Class Discussion

When do you make complaints? If there are more ideas or students come up with other ideas, you can add them to the list.

1. When a delivery is too late
2. When a person does not keep their promise
3. When service was not good (attitude of the staff)
4. When there is a defect in a product
5. When a payment is delayed

What could be an ideal way to make a complaint?

1. Avoid being too aggressive
2. Explain the problem in detail and clearly
3. Demand or request some specific action that you want them to take

When making a complaint, what kind of actions can you request?

1. Refund/exchange/replacement
2. Sending an expert in that area to solve the problem
3. Compensation

My Own Dialogue

Choose a situation where you need to handle a complaint:

_____

Choose a reason why you got the complaint:

_____

Choose a resolution for the complaint:

_____

Based on the above selections, make your own dialogue.

A:

B:

A:

B:

A:

B:

Act Out

Act out your own dialogue in front of the class. You can get help from your partner if you need a dialogue partner.

Teacher's Model Dialogue

Ms. Hyland is calling Ms. Hathrow to make a complaint about her late payment.

A: Good afternoon, this is Ella Hathrow at ABC Company. What can I do for you?

B: Hi, Ms. Hathrow. I'm calling to tell you that your flight ticket payment is overdue. I'm sorry, but you promised me that you would pay it by last Friday, but it has still not been transferred to our account. It's now three days late.

B: I see. I'm very sorry about that. The problem was caused by my bank system which kept giving me the message that my security codes are wrong. I could not handle the problem right away since the bank is closed during the weekend.

A: OK, then could you transfer the airfare amount as soon as possible? If you do not pay immediately, the flight will be canceled automatically. I'm concerned that you will not get the flight time that you want since it's high season.

B: I assure you, Ms. Hyland, that I will transfer right away. Sorry for the inconvenience.

Chapter 07

Orders

Sales Related Calls

In business situations, you may have to place or take an order by telephone. Let's learn the expressions and phrases regarding sales related calls in English.

📷 SNAPSHOT

Let's learn key vocabulary/phrases you would use when giving or receiving an order by telephone.

give an order	sales	check	double-check	statement
purchase specifications	seller	buyer	make a contract	money

🔍 TODAY'S SITUATION

Ms. Rose Park, a cheese importer in Seoul, is phoning her New Zealand supplier Mr. Kim to place an order. Let's learn the sentence patterns and key expressions.

A: I'd like to place an order for nine large boxes of Gouda if you can, and five small boxes.

B: We are OK for the large, but we've only got three small boxes of Gouda in stock at the moment. Would you like the rest later?

A: No, we'll take those three boxes and forget about the rest. Now, have you got any low-fat Gouda in stock? About five boxes?

B: Yes, we have. You ordered Gouda: nine large boxes, three small, and five of low-fat. Anything else?

A: No, that's all for now.

B: OK then. Could you re-send the order by e-mail as soon as possible? I need it for the export papers.

 Check Point

- 주문하는 표현: **I'd like to place an order for A.**
  A를 주문하고 싶습니다.

- 재고가 있는지 묻는 표현: **Have you got A in stock?**
  A 물건의 재고가 있습니까?

- 더 주문할 것이 있는지 묻는 표현: **Anything else?**
  더 주문하실 것 있습니까?

- 주문할 것이 더 이상 없음을 나타내는 표현: **That's all for now.**
  그것이 전부입니다.

Further Expressions

- 주문하는 표현: A를 주문하고 싶습니다.
  - I'd like to place an order for A.
  - I want to order A.
  - Can/May I place an order for A?
  - Could I give an order for A?

- 더 주문할 것이 있는지 묻는 표현: 더 주문하실 것 있습니까?
  - Anything else?
  - Is there anything else?
  - Is there anything else you want to add to that?
  - Do you need anything else?

- 주문할 것이 더 이상 없음을 나타내는 표현: 그것이 전부입니다.
  - That's all for now.
  - That's all that I want/need.
  - That's all.
  - That's it.

🔍 PATTERN PRACTICE

Practice with a Partner

Let's practice the dialogue patterns and expressions that you have just learned with your partner.

A:

B:

A:

B:

A:

B:

EXTRA EXPRESSIONS

A: We've only got A in stock at the moment.
We've only had A in stock for a while now.
We've only kept A in stock for a while.

B: Could you re-send the order by e-mail?
Could you re-send the order by telephone?
Could you re-send the order by mail?
Could you re-send the order by fax?

PRACTICE BY YOURSELF

1. Vocabulary Check-up

Match the words with the correct definition.

1. stock • • A what is left after everything or everyone else has gone, been used, dealt with, or mentioned

2. Gouda • • B a supply of a particular type of thing that a shop has available to sell

3. rest • • C the business of selling and sending goods to other countries

4. export • • D a yellow Dutch cheese that does not have a very strong taste

5. supplier • • E a company or person that provides a particular product

Complete the sentence with a proper word. Change the form if needed.

1. I want to learn how to make _____ because it is my favorite cheese.

2. The government made a law banning the _____ of toxic waste.

3. We have a huge _____ of quality carpets on sale.

4. The company is famous for being the UK's largest _____ of office equipment.

5. You carry these two bags, and I'll bring the _____.

2. Sentence Paraphrasing

> Practice other sentences out loud keeping the same meaning with the given sentence.

❶ I'd like to place an order for A.

❷ Anything else?

❸ That's all for now.

Telephoning Etiquette & Tips in Business

1. **When placing an order by phone:** It's important to confirm your order by some kind of written document such as email or fax if you made the order through a phone call. Phone calls can cause misunderstandings, and they also do not assure your order unless the company has a recording system for the phone calls. Otherwise, you can ask the person who got the order to acknowledge your order by fax or email.

2. **When making sales calls:** You need to get the customers' attention in 15 seconds or less. Create excitement. You have a fantastic product that will make a great improvement in your customer's lives. You're about to give people on the other end of the line a huge present by telling them about this wonderful product. Make sure that energy and enthusiasm come across in your tone of voice. Also, offer the prospect something useful regardless of whether or not they buy your product. If the prospect won't talk, ask about a better time to call back. Close every single call, even if the prospect seems completely uninterested.

MAKE MY OWN DIALOGUE

Idea Bank

How did you place an order by phone?

1. Have you ever placed an order by phone? How was the experience? (You can think about the latest or most unforgettable experience.)

- What products or services did you order?

  · home supplies

  · food

  _____

- In what manner did the receiver handle the call?

  · very kind and friendly, _____

- Was it convenient to place an order by phone? Why or why not?

  · not convenient, since I needed to spell out every single letter of my name and address

  · not convenient, since I needed to conduct the payment separately

  _____

2. Would you like a job taking orders on the phone? Why or why not?

- Yes, because I can get the orders immediately with the way I persuade the customers. I can see the sales going up because of my effort.

- No, I do not like talking on the phone with someone that I do not know. It makes me uncomfortable.

  _____

Class Discussion

What kind of products or services do you order by phone? If there are more ideas or students come up with other ideas, you can add them to the list.

1. office supplies
2. furniture
3. home shopping products

What are some other ways to place orders? Which one do you prefer? Why?

1. On site visiting: I can see the products with my eyes, so I can choose the product that I want.
2. Online shopping: It saves time, there are a variety of products, and it's usually much cheaper.

What kind of information should you include when placing an order by phone?

1. Product – quantity, quality, model, pattern, color
2. Delivery date – delivery location, warehousing
3. Delivery method – packing, special markings, shipping instructions
4. Payment method – credit card, cash, discounts

My Own Dialogue

Choose a product that you will be placing an order for:
_____

Write down the details of the products that you would like to place an order for:
_____

Based on the above selections, make your own dialogue.

A:

B:

A:

B:

A:

B:

Act Out

Act out your own dialogue in front of the class. You can get help from your partner if you need a dialogue partner.

Teacher's Model Dialogue

Ms. Hathrow is placing an order for office furniture by phone.

A: Office Furniture. This is Lee. How can I help you?

B: Yes, I'd like to place an order. Do I need to call the customer representative number?

A: No, I'll be happy to help you now. What is your name, please?

B: My name is Ella Hathrow, and I'm with ABC Company.

A: Oh, I remember ABC having a prior order last month. What would you like to order?

B: We need to order 10 more chairs and a meeting table as well. The models are same as the ones we placed last time.

A: So you want them at the same address, and by when do you need the products?

B: Yes. We want them on the fifth floor conference room. Is it possible to get them this week?

A: Sure, we will try our best to send them as soon as possible. Who should be invoiced?

B: Send the bill to our accounts payable division. They will handle the payment.

Chapter 08 Agreement

Reaching Agreement

During a business telephone call, you may encounter disagreements, so you should know how to deal with these situations and reach agreements. Let's learn some expressions and phrases regarding reaching agreements in English.

📷 SNAPSHOT

Let's learn key vocabulary/phrases you have in mind when thinking about agreements.

arguing	discussion	time-off	cooperation	negotiation
logic	reasoning	agree	disagree	alternatives
short-cut				

_____   _____
_____   _____

🔍 TODAY'S SITUATION

Susan calls the reception desk to ask about her luggage. She gets an unexpected answer regarding her suitcase but finds an alternative. Let's learn the sentence patterns and key expressions.

A: Oh, hello? This is Susan in room 153. Would it be possible to leave my suitcase at the reception after check-out?

B: I'm sorry it is not possible. It is our hotel policy.

A: Oh, really? That is a totally unexpected answer. Then, what am I supposed to do? I want to put my luggage somewhere safe until I have to go to the airport.

B: Instead, you can use a locker in the hotel lobby to store your luggage after check-out. But please don't leave anything valuable in it.

A: No, of course not. Can I pay my fee by credit card?

B: Sorry? You can't be serious! You can use the locker for free.

✏️ Check Point

- 반대/거절 의사를 나타내는 표현: **I'm sorry it is not possible.**
  죄송하지만 불가능합니다.

- 주변 사람의 자문을 구하는 표현: **What am I supposed to do?**
  제가 어떻게 하면 될까요?

- 대안을 나타내는 표현: **: Instead, ~**
  ~대신에

- 상대방의 의견에 놀람을 나타내는 표현: **Sorry? You can't be serious!**
  뭐라고요? 농담이시죠?

💬 Further Expressions

- 반대/거절 의사를 나타내는 표현: 죄송하지만 불가능합니다.
  - I'm sorry it is not possible/feasible.
  - I'm afraid you can't.
  - I don't think/believe it is possible.
  - I (totally/completely/entirely) disagree with A.

- 대안을 나타내는 표현: 대신에, / B에 대한 대안은 A입니다.
  - Instead,
  - An alternative of B is A.
  - A is an alternative to B.

- 상대방의 의견에 놀람을 나타내는 표현: 뭐라고요? 농담이시죠?
  - Sorry? You can't be serious!
  - Are you serious?
  - You've got to be kidding!

🔍 PATTERN PRACTICE

Practice with a Partner

Let's practice the dialogue patterns and expressions that you have just learned with your partner.

A:

B:

A:

B:

A:

B:

EXTRA EXPRESSIONS

A: What <u>am</u> I <u>supposed to</u> do?
What <u>am</u> I <u>expected to</u> do?
What <u>should</u> I do?
What do you think I <u>ought to</u> do?

A: No, of course not.
Certainly not.
Not at all.
No way.

🔍 PRACTICE BY YOURSELF

1. Vocabulary Check-up

Match the words with the correct definition.

❶ reception • • Ⓐ to say what someone should or should not do, especially because of rules or what someone in authority has said

❷ check-out • • Ⓑ without having to pay

❸ be supposed to • • Ⓒ the desk or office where visitors arriving in a hotel or large organization go first

❹ for free • • Ⓓ the time by which you must leave a hotel room

❺ alternative • • Ⓔ something you can choose to do or use instead of something else

Complete the sentence with a proper word. Change the form if needed.

❶ Please leave your key at the _____ desk.

❷ _____ is at noon.

❸ The camera is under warranty, so we'll fix it _____.

❹ We _____ check out of the hotel by 11 o'clock.

❺ I had no _____ but to report him to the police.

2. Sentence Paraphrasing

> Practice other sentences out loud keeping the same meaning with the given sentence.

❶ I'm sorry, but it is not possible.

❷ Sorry? You can't be serious!

❸ What am I supposed to do?

Telephoning Etiquette & Tips in Business

1. *Advantages of telephone calls over emails:* There are many reasons why telephone calls are a better and more effective communication channel than emails for businesses. One of the main reasons why picking up the phone and calling someone is better than sending an email, is the fact that any issues can be dealt with faster and more efficiently. Another important reason is that key information and content can remain in context during phone calls, whereas misunderstandings can often occur in emails. If the subject matter of a conversation is of a complicated, technical, or particularly sensitive nature, an email can often lead to unnecessary confusion and misunderstanding, leading to long and drawn out email exchanges. Finally, phoning colleagues, partners, suppliers, customers, and contacts can prove much more effective in terms of relationship building, networking, and maintaining quality communication streams between all parties.

MAKE MY OWN DIALOGUE

Idea Bank

How do you reach an agreement when there is an objection?

Let's compare how you handle disagreements at your workplace and in your personal life.

At the workplace

❶ Who did you have a disagreement with?

❷ What was it in regard to?

❸ How did you handle the disagreement?

In the personal setting

❶ Who did you have a disagreement with?

❷ What was it in regard to?

❸ How did you handle the disagreement?

The big difference between the two types of disagreement is

_____

_____

Class Discussion

What could be causes of disagreements at work? If there are more ideas or students come up with other ideas, you can add them to the list.

1. Personality difference (different point of view, different values, differing interests)
2. Poor communication/misunderstanding
3. Failure to appreciate cultural differences
4. Poor performance/lack of commitment
5. Unrealistic demands

How do you handle disagreements? How can you reach an agreement?

1. Acknowledge that there will be differing perceptions on an issue
2. Make a clear statement of why you have that opinion and how it could lead to the goal
3. Stress mutual interest in making a deal

Do you think having a disagreement is bad? Why or why not?

1. It's good to have a disagreement because it reveals differences which need to be resolved.
2. It's not good to have a disagreement since a disagreement on a certain issue can lead to a bad relationship.

My Own Dialogue

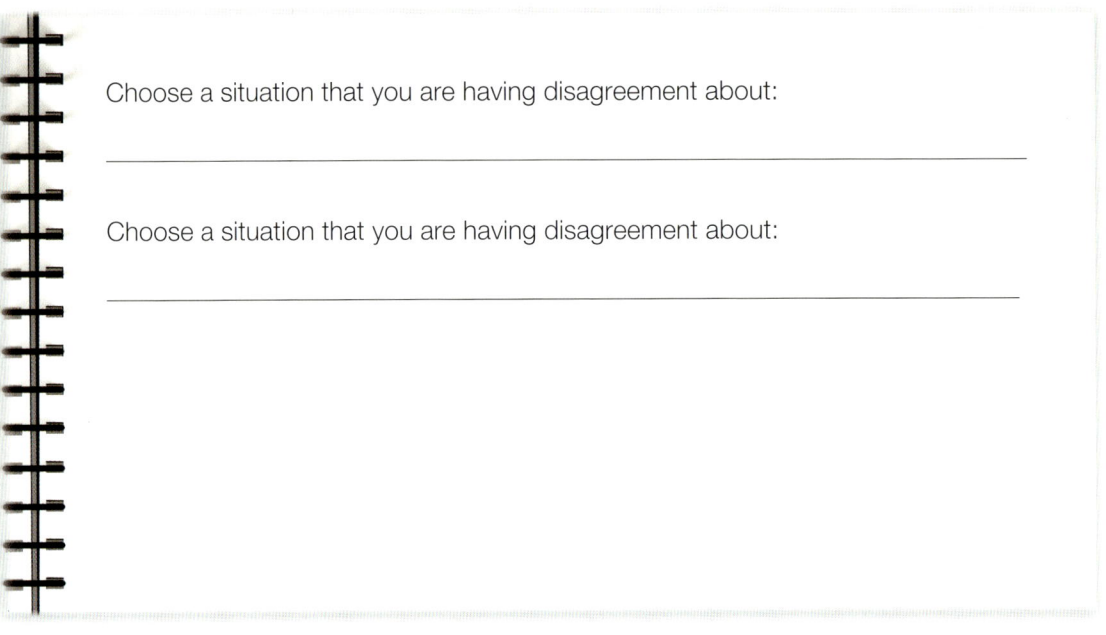

Choose a situation that you are having disagreement about:
_____

Choose a situation that you are having disagreement about:
_____

 Based on the above selections, make your own dialogue.

A:

B:

A:

B:

A:

B:

Act Out

Act out your own dialogue in front of the class. You can get help from your partner if you need a dialogue partner.

Teacher's Model Dialogue

Ms. Hathrow is having a disagreement over deciding a meeting place with Mr. Richard.

A: Mr. Richard, I'm calling to discuss where we should pick for the meeting place with S&E. I've sent you emails regarding this matter, but you don't seem to be reading them.

B: What do you mean by that? Are you saying that I just ignored your opinions?

A: I apologize for the misunderstanding, I didn't mean that. Let's just get into our issue. I don't think our meeting room is appropriate for the meeting with S&E. There will be twenty people who will be attending, and it's almost lunch time as well.

B: So are you saying we need to find a place where we can have a luncheon?

A: Exactly, that's why I recommended the Smith's since it has a large space where everybody can fit comfortably, and it has a projector and computer, so we can have the meeting, and moreover, we can have lunch there.

B: But I have a meeting at 2:00 at the office, so I will be in a rush. That's why I wanted to have the meeting in our meeting room with the food catered.

A: Oh, I totally forgot that you mentioned that. I fully understand. How about moving your agenda for the meeting to the first order of business? Then you can leave right after you finish.

B: That sounds good. I think we've both got a good deal.

Chapter 09

Wrap Up

Ending a Conversation

You need to know how to end a conversation politely on the phone. Let's learn the expressions and phrases regarding wrapping up a conversation in English.

📷 SNAPSHOT

Let's learn key vocabulary/phrases you would use when ending a conversation on the phone.

Bye.	Good bye.	See you later.	miss	follow up
I need to go.	another call	busy schedule	time to go	hurry

_____   _____

_____   _____

🔍 TODAY'S SITUATION

Here are four situations that end a conversation on the phone. Let's learn the sentence patterns and key expressions.

A: Thank you for calling. Good bye.

B: OK. Bye.

A: I'm having lunch now. Call me back in an hour, OK?

B: Sure. Bye.

A: Ron, I'm talking to a client. Would you mind calling me back this afternoon?

B: Of course not. I'll call you after lunch. Bye.

A: I can't talk right now. I'm driving. I'll call you right back. Bye.

B: OK. Good bye.

✎ Check Point

- 전화 통화에 대해 고마움을 나타내는 표현: **Thank you for calling.**
  전화해 주셔서 감사합니다.

- 다음에 다시 통화 하자고 나타내는 표현: **Call me back. /**
  Would you mind calling me back? /
  I'll call you right back.
  다음에 다시 전화 통화 하자.

- 전화를 끊을 때 사용하는 표현: **Good bye. / Bye.**
  안녕히 계세요.

💬 Further Expressions

- 전화 통화에 대해 고마움을 나타내는 표현: 전화해 주셔서 감사합니다.
  - Thank you for calling.
  - I appreciate your call.
  - I am grateful you called.

- 다음에 다시 통화 하자고 나타내는 표현: 다음에 다시 전화 통화 하자.
  - Call me back.
  - Would you mind calling me back?
  - I'll call you right back.
  - Can you call me back?
  - May I call you back?

- 지금 당장 전화 할 수 없음을 나타내는 이유 표현
  - I'm having lunch now. 지금 점심식사 중입니다.
  - I'm talking to a client. 고객과 상담 중입니다.
  - I'm driving. 운전 중입니다.
  - I'm terribly sorry, but I need to go to a meeting immediately.
    죄송하지만 지금 바로 회의에 참석해야 합니다.
  - I'm sorry, but I'm getting on a plane. 죄송하지만 비행기에 탑승해야 합니다.

🔍 PATTERN PRACTICE

Practice with a Partner

Let's practice the dialogue patterns and expressions that you have just learned with your partner.

A:

B:

A:

B:

A:

B:

EXTRA EXPRESSIONS

A: Call me back <u>in an hour</u>.
Call me back <u>after an hour</u>.
Call me back <u>this afternoon</u>.
Call me <u>right back</u>.
Call me back <u>later</u>.

A: Would you mind calling me back this afternoon?
Would you mind <u>postponing</u> the meeting?
<u>Do you mind</u> opening the window?

🔍 PRACTICE BY YOURSELF

1. Vocabulary Check-up

Match the words with the correct definition.

① wrap up • • Ⓐ to telephone somebody again or to telephone somebody who telephoned you earlier

② call back • • Ⓑ to change the date or time of a planned event or action to a later one

③ grateful • • Ⓒ You do or deal with the last part of something, so that there is no more for you to do or deal with.

④ postpone • • Ⓓ feeling that you want to thank someone because of something kind thing that they have done, or showing this feeling

⑤ follow up • • Ⓔ to take further action about something

Complete the sentences with a the proper word. Change the form if needed.

① Let's _____ the meeting, and take a break.

② I'm so _____ for all your help.

③ The match had to be _____ until next week due to bad weather.

④ _____ in half an hour, and then he'll answer the phone.

⑤ The police will _____ all possible clues.

2. Sentence Paraphrasing

Practice other sentences out loud keeping the same meaning with the given sentence.

❶ Thank you for calling.

❷ Call me back.

❸ Good bye.

Telephoning Etiquette & Tips in Business

1. *Ending telephone calls* : Ending telephone calls can be difficult. Calls can easily go on too long. Alternatively, they can finish too quickly and seem unprofessional. It is important to listen for signals showing that the other person is ready to close the call. Also you should make that signal as well. End on a positive note and do not put down the receiver too quickly as it may seem rude. Hang up gently. Never slam the receiver in the other person's ear.

2. *Say "Thank you"* : Thanking your caller is a great prelude to saying goodbye. It is an effective social cue to closing a conversation. A "thank you closing" allows you to respectfully validate their time and input but also indicates that the dialog is now complete. End the conversation with agreement on what is to happen next; if you are to follow-up, do so immediately.

MAKE MY OWN DIALOGUE

Idea Bank

How do you usually end a conversation on the phone?

Let's compare how you end conversations on the phone. Think about some calls that you made recently.

Business Call

1. How long was the call?

2. Why did you need to end the call?

3. What was the signal for ending the call?

4. Which phrases did you use for an ending?

Personal Call

1. How long was the call?

2. Why did you need to end the call?

3. What was the signal for ending the call?

4. Which phrases did you use for an ending?

The big difference between the two call endings is

_____

_____

Class Discussion

What are the reasons for ending a call? If there are more ideas or students come up with other ideas, you can add them to the list.

1. When the discussion is finished
2. When an agreement between the two are made
3. When a person has another meeting or is busy with other work

What could be done before ending a call?

1. Confirmation on the discussed topic
2. Promising action
3. Thanking

What could be considered bad manners when ending a call?

1. Just hanging up without saying sorry when someone dialed the wrong number
2. Ending the call without saying goodbye. Even if you're ending the call on bad terms. It's always best to say, "I'm sorry, but I must end this call now."

My Own Dialogue

Choose a situation when you are ending a call:

_____

Choose an issue that has been discussed and confirmed before ending the call:

_____

Based on the above selections, make your own dialogue.

A:

B:

A:

B:

A:

B:

Act Out

Act out your own dialogue in front of the class. You can get help from your partner if you need a dialogue partner.

Teacher's Model Dialogue

Ms. Hathrow is ending a call with Mr. Richard.

A: Mr. Richard, let me quickly go over what we discussed again. So the meeting that was originally planned for Friday has been postponed to Tuesday at 2:00. Is that right?

B: Yes, I'll send you an email for confirmation. I'm sorry about having to change our schedule.

A: It's no problem. Actually, I'm working on a project now, and this Friday is also busy for me.

B: Thank you for your understanding. I look forward to seeing you next week. And if you have any questions or changes to be made, give me a call any time.

A: I will. Is there anything else that we need to discuss? Otherwise, I'm sorry but I have to go. The other line is ringing.

B: No, see you on Tuesday!

Chapter 10: Calling Back

Keeping Posted

In business situations, you may have to call clients back to keep them posted on issues. Let's learn some expressions and phrases regarding calling people back in English.

📷 SNAPSHOT

Let's learn key vocabulary/phrases you would use in calling back situations.

As I mentioned before,	call again	acquaintance
common issues	unsolved problems	steady
keep posted	check the progress	
_____	_____	
_____	_____	

🔍 TODAY'S SITUATION

Anne calls back Peter to keep him posted on his company anniversary. Let's learn the sentence patterns and key expressions.

A: Good afternoon. This is Anne from A&G event agency. Is this Peter?

B: Oh, yes. We spoke last Monday, didn't we? Do you have any special offers for our upcoming 20th anniversary of the company?

A: Absolutely. That's why I am calling. Well, you mentioned some sort of after-dinner entertainment, didn't you? I've got up-to-date news for you.

B: Oh, really? As I said before, I am looking for somewhere a bit exotic to have a drink and dance as well but also somewhere comfortable where we can just sit and chat with colleagues.

A: Perfect. How about ABC Hotel garden and outdoor pool? The hotel recently finished reconstruction. It's usually really popular with our business clients, and we have a very good DJ.

B: That sounds great. Perfect.

✏️ Check Point

- 이전에 말한 화제에 이어 이야기를 시작하는 표현:
  Well, you mentioned A. / As I said before, ~.
  음, 당신이 A를 언급했었죠. / 제가 이전에 말한 것과 같이, ~.

- 정보를 확인하는 표현: **We spoke last Monday, didn't we? / Well, you mentioned some sort of after-dinner entertainment, didn't you?**
  우리 지난 월요일에 얘기했었죠, 그렇죠? / 음, 당신이 저녁 식사 후 오락의 종류에 대해 언급했었죠, 맞죠?

- 최신정보/소식을 전달하는 표현: **I've got up-to-date news for you.**
  당신을 위해 최신 소식을 가져왔습니다.

- 상대의 말에 긍정적으로 응답하는 표현: **That sounds great.**
  정말 멋지군요.

💬 Further Expressions

- 이전에 말한 화제에 이어 이야기를 시작하는 표현
    - **Well, you mentioned A.** 음, 당신이 A를 언급했었죠.
    - **As I said before, ~.** 제가 이전에 말한 것과 같이, ~.
    - **As I previously stated, ~.**
    - **You'll remember that I said earlier that ~.**
    - **As stated previously, ~.**

- 최신정보/소식을 전달하는 표현: 당신을 위해 최신 소식을 가져왔습니다.
    - **I've got up-to-date/the newest/the latest/red-hot news for you.**
    - **I want to tell you the latest news.**

- 상대의 말에 긍정적으로 응답하는 표현: 정말 멋지군요.
    - **That sounds (really/absolutely) great.**
    - **Sounds great/nice/good.**
    - **Perfect.**

PATTERN PRACTICE

Practice with a Partner

Let's practice the dialogue patterns and expressions that you have just learned with your partner.

A:

B:

A:

B:

A:

B:

EXTRA EXPRESSIONS

A: Absolutely
Certainly.
Surely.
Of course.
Why not?

A: That's why I am calling.
I like ice cream. That's why I eat ice cream a lot.
(cf.) I like ice cream. That's because it is sweet.

🔍 PRACTICE BY YOURSELF

1. Vocabulary Check-up

Match the words with the correct definition.

1. upcoming • • A. to make sure that somebody is safe, happy, etc. or that something is progressing as it should be

2. anniversary • • B. happening soon

3. keep somebody posted • • C. including all the latest information

4. check on • • D. a date on which something special or important happened in a previous year

5. up-to-date • • E. keep somebody informed

Complete the sentences with a the proper word. Change the form if needed.

1. They have access to _____ information through a computer database.

2. June and Kim celebrated their twentieth wedding _____ in July.

3. Which candidate do you support in the _____ election?

4. I will _____ you _____ on how it goes.

5. Dr. Jack, did you _____ all my patients?

2. Sentence Paraphrasing

> Practice other sentences out loud keeping the same meaning with the given sentence.

❶ As I said before, ~.

❷ I want to tell you the latest news.

❸ Sounds great.

Telephoning Etiquette & Tips in Business

1. **Handling missed calls:** Modern technology allows us to never miss another call again. Voice mail systems and mobile phones' 'missed calls' feature saves us the trouble of wondering who called us and when. That leaves us no reason to NOT give a call back. Common sense tells us to return a missed call as soon as possible. Ideally, you must return a call within a 24 hour period. Unless a voicemail is left with a specific time and date, try to call back as soon as you can.

2. **In the case of disconnection:** Call back if you are disconnected from a call you placed. It's your responsibility to call back.

3. **Things to avoid when using cell phones:** It can be easy to glance at your phone in the midst of a conversation to check the time or confirm if someone is calling you. Never look at your phone while in any conversation. If you must glance at your phone, wait for a break in the conversation, or if there isn't one, hold up your hand and say "excuse me," check your phone, and then apologize and encourage the other party to continue. Also do not take your personal calls during work. Last, do not leave phone sounds or ringers on. That might disturb others.

MAKE MY OWN DIALOGUE

Idea Bank

How do you handle missed calls?

Let's compare how you handle missed calls.

Business Call	Personal Call
❶ Do you have many missed calls? Why or why not?	❶ Do you have many missed calls? Why or why not?
❷ When you check the missed calls, how fast do you return the call?	❷ When you check the missed calls, how fast do you return the call?
❸ Which calls don't you return? Why?	❸ Which calls don't you return? Why?
❹ Which phrases do you use for calling back?	❹ Which phrases do you use for calling back?

The big difference between the two types of missed call is

_____

_____

Class Discussion

What are the reasons for having missed calls? If there are more ideas or students come up with other ideas, you can add them to the list.

1. When I was in a meeting
2. When I had my cell phone on mute
3. When I was out of the office for business trips or vacations

___

What are signals for letting someone know to call you back?

1. Leaving messages with the receiver
2. Leaving voicemails
3. Sending an email or text message

___

On what occasions do people want to get a return call?

1. When they want an answer or reply that they could not get right away
2. When they want to know the progress of ongoing matters.
3. When the receiver is not the person who's in charge

___

My Own Dialogue

Choose a situation when you are calling someone back:
_____

Choose a person who you're having a conversation with:
_____

Choose a topic that you are discussing during the return call:
_____

Based on the above selections, make your own dialogue.

A:

B:

A:

B:

A:

B:

Act Out

Act out your own dialogue in front of the class. You can get help from your partner if you need a dialogue partner.

Teacher's Model Dialogue

Ms. Hathrow is returning a call from Mr. Richard.

A: Mr. Richard, this is Ella Hathrow. I got a message that you called, so I'm returning your call.

B: Hi, Ms. Hathrow. Thanks for getting back to me so soon. What I wanted to talk about was the interview schedule for the new employee hiring.

A: Oh, I see. I guess I didn't reply to your email. Let me check, I was writing about…. Oops, it's still in my mail box. Sorry. I'm extremely busy this week so it will be hard to fit in the time that you suggested. How about delaying the interview until next week?

B: It should be done early next week. Otherwise, the hiring process gets too long. But as I mentioned, you must be the interviewer since we are hiring your coworker.

A: Of course. I assure you that I will be involved in the interview next week. Well, I have one more question, though. Do you have time now to talk about the candidates' resume?

B: Actually, I have an appointment. Let me call you back.

A: No problem. Talk to you soon.

Part II
Socializing

Chapter 11: Introduction & Greeting

Formal Introduction & Getting to Know Someone

In business situations, you may meet some foreign visitors and need to know how to introduce yourself and your colleagues to them and also how to greet foreign guests. Let's learn how we introduce ourselves and say hello in English.

📷 SNAPSHOT

Let's learn key vocabulary/phrases you would use in introductions and greeting situations.

say hello	a business card	handshakes	suit
first impression	Let me introduce	yourself	courtesy
making eye contact	smile		

🔍 TODAY'S SITUATION

Mr. Blanks visits a customer's company. He introduces himself and says hello to Ms. Placid and Mr. Evans. Let's learn the sentence patterns and key expressions.

A: Hello. I'd like to introduce myself to you. I'm David Blanks, and I'm a marketing manager at S&E.

B: Hello, Mr. Blanks. I'm Lydia Placid. Have you met John Evans? This is my partner John Evans, a sales manager for Moontech. (hold out a hand to shake)

A: Nice to meet you, Ms. Placid and Mr. Evans. Thank you for taking the time to meet with me today.

B: It's our pleasure. And please, call us Lydia and John. How long have you been working for S&E?

A: For about 7 years, since graduating from college. How about you?

B: I've been working here for 6 years, since 2008.

✏️ Check Point

- 자기 소개를 시작하는 표현: **I'd like to introduce myself.**
  제 소개를 하고 싶습니다.

- 동료 소개를 시작하는 표현: **Have you met A?**
  당신은 A를 만나본 적이 있습니까?

- 동료를 소개하는 표현: **This is my partner/colleague/coworker A.**
  이 사람은 제 동료인 A입니다.

- 근무 기간을 묻는 표현: **How long have you been working for A?**
  A에서 얼마나 오랫동안 근무하고 있습니까?

- 근무 기간에 대해 대답하는 표현: **I have been working here for A.**
  저는 이곳에서 A기간동안 근무하고 있습니다.

💬 Further Expressions

- 자기 소개를 시작하는 표현: 제 소개를 하고 싶습니다.
  - I'd like to introduce myself.
  - Let me introduce myself.
  - May I introduce myself?
  - Allow me to introduce myself.

- 동료 소개를 시작하는 표현: 당신은 A를 만나본 적이 있습니까?
  - Have you (formally) met A?
  - Have you ever been introduced to A?

- 근무 기간에 대해 대답하는 표현
  - **I have been working here for A.** 저는 이곳에서 A (기간) 동안 근무하고 있습니다.
  - **I have worked here for A.** 저는 이곳에서 A (기간) 동안 근무하고 있습니다.
  - **I have been working here since A.** 저는 이곳에서 A (시간)부터 현재까지 일하고 있습니다.
  - **I have worked here since A.** 저는 이곳에서 A (시간) 부터 현재까지 일하고 있습니다.

🔍 PATTERN PRACTICE

Practice with a Partner

Let's practice the dialogue patterns and expressions that you have just learned with your partner.

A:

B:

A:

B:

A:

B:

EXTRA EXPRESSIONS

A: Thank you for taking the time to meet with me today.
Thank you for taking the time to speak with me.
Thank you for the time you spent with me.

B: It's our pleasure.
It's a pleasure.
Don't mention it.
You're welcome.

PRACTICE BY YOURSELF

1. Vocabulary Check-up

Match the words with the correct definition.

1. courtesy • • A to hold something such as your hand, or something in your hand, in front of you towards somebody else

2. hold out • • B to complete their studies successfully and leave their school or university

3. graduate from • • C very correctly and seriously, and is used especially in official situations

4. colleague • • D politeness, respect, and consideration for others

5. formally • • E the person you work with, especially in a professional job

Complete the sentences with the proper word. Change the form if needed.

1. You must be David, the man said, _____ his hand.

2. Mary _____ turned down the proposal due to fatal errors.

3. William doesn't like his _____ who does not lift a finger.

4. I _____ Harvard Law School.

5. Andrew must be a gentleman who behaves with the utmost _____ towards ladies.

2. Sentence Paraphrasing

> Practice some other sentences out loud, keeping the same meaning with the given sentence.

❶ I'd like to introduce myself.

❷ Have you formally met A?

❸ It's my pleasure.

Culture Tips on Introduction & Greeting

1. *Introduction order :* In social situations, a man is traditionally introduced to a woman. However, in the business world, introductions are based on a person's rank or position in an organization. Whoever is the highest-ranking person is introduced to everyone else first and all others in order of their positions. If you introduce two people of equal rank to each other, introduce the one you know less well to the one you know best.

2. *Greetings :* Most Western countries make solid eye contact and offer a firm handshake. In Asian cultures, greetings are done by bowing your head slightly and keeping handshakes lighter and less firm. Too much eye contact in Asian cultures is considered rude. Latin American cultures tend to operate on a slower timetable than Western and Asian cultures.

MAKE MY OWN DIALOGUE

Idea Bank

How would you introduce yourself to a person that you first meet?

1. How would you like to be called by someone you meet for the first time?

- Mr. _____ / Ms. _____
- by your first name

_____

2. How long have you been working in this company/field/department?

- I have been working in ABC company for 7 years.
- I have been working in the finance field for 7 years.
- I have been working in accounting/finance/marketing/human resources/R&D for 7 years.

_____

3. What is your position, and what kind of job responsibility do you have?

- I'm an assistant manager, and I deal with accounts payable.
- I'm a manager, and I'm in responsible for new business development.
- I'm a general manager, and I'm in charge of marketing strategies.

_____

Class Discussion

Discuss some occasions where you usually meet business partners. and Practice introducing yourself or your colleagues. If there are more ideas or students come up with other ideas, you can add them up onto the list

1. meeting (state specific kinds: negotiation, IR meeting, alliance meeting)
2. conference/seminar/show/exhibition
3. _____

Discuss the background information that you can use for the introduction of someone or yourself which could make it easier for them to start a conversation.

1. common interest (hobbies, spare time activities)
2. a place they both know well (He has been doing business in Latin America for 10 years.)
3. a person they both know (He has been a great partner with Mr. Kim for 10 years.)
4. _____

Discuss the rank or authority in a business setting.

1. Who is of greater rank or authority?
   - Your boss or your colleague?
   - Your senior colleague or junior colleague?
   - Your customer/client or your employee?

 In a business setting, the position determines rank first, and after that comes gender, and then age. For social introductions, men are usually introduced to women, as a sign of respect. Gender is not a factor in business settings, where rank is more important.

My Own Dialogue

Choose one place where you met someone to make introduction:
_____

Choose a person accompanying you:
_____

Choose a person that you met at the place:
_____

Choose some background information that you can offer to make the two people start the conversation:
_____

Based on the above selections, make your own dialogue.

A:

B:

A:

B:

A:

B:

Act Out

Act out your dialogue in front of the class. You can get help from your partner if you need a dialogue partner.

Teacher's Model Dialogue

Ms. Placid is attending the Global Marketing Conference accompanied by Mr. Houston, a vice president of Moontech. They meet Mr. Blanks, a marketing manager at S&E, at the conference booth.

A: (seeing Mr. Blanks at S&E booth) Excuse me, are you Mr. Blanks? I'm Lydia Placid from Moontech.

B: Oh, Ms. Placid. It's great to see you here.

A: Well, Mr. Blanks, I would like to introduce our vice president, Mr. Houston. He has worked in our company for 15 years, and he is an expert in the field of marketing. And Mr. Houston, this is Thomas Blanks, a marketing manager at S&E. He has been working at S&E since 2010 and has begun business with us last year.

B: How do you do, Mr. Houston? I've read many news articles on your marketing strategies and was very much impressed.

C: How do you do, Mr. Blanks? It's our pleasure to see you here. Hope to see you back at our Supplier's Night.

B: Sure. How long are you planning to stay at the conference? I would like to talk to you more, but I need to prepare a speech for the next session.

A: Actually, we will be attending the next session, and then we will have a meeting with our client.

B: It was a pleasure to meet you here, and I hope to see you soon.

A,C: Goodbye. It's a pleasure to have met you.

Chapter 12

Welcoming

Receiving Visitors

At the workplace, you might have foreign visitors come to see you for diverse reasons. Let's learn how we can welcome these visitors in English.

📷 SNAPSHOT

Let's learn key vocabulary/phrases you would use in a welcoming situation.

welcome	visit	show around	reception
show room	meeting room	look around	flight
trip journey	business card		

_____   _____

_____   _____

🔍 TODAY'S SITUATION

Mr. Blanks visits a customer's company, Moontech for the first time and meets Ms. Placid. Let's learn the sentence patterns and key expressions.

A: Good morning. Please, come in. Are you Mr. Blanks?

B: Yes, I am. Are you Ms. Placid?

A: Yes, I'm Lydia Placid. Welcome to Moontech. It's nice to finally meet you in person.

B: Thank you. I've been very much looking forward to this visit. It's great to meet you, too.

A: Please have a seat, and make yourself comfortable. You mentioned that it's your first time visiting our office. Did you have any trouble finding the place/office/building?

B: No, the directions you sent me were very clear, and there was hardly any traffic.

A: Can I get you something to drink?

B: Coffee, please.

Chapter 12 Welcoming

✏️ Check Point

- 신분을 확인하는 표현: **Are you A?**
  당신이 A입니까?

- 방문객을 환영하는 표현: **Welcome to A.**
  A에 방문하신 것을 환영합니다.

- 만나서 반갑다는 표현: **It's nice to meet you in person, It's great to meet you.**
  당신을 만나서 반갑습니다

- 상대방에게 음료를 제안하는 표현: **Can I get you something to drink?**
  마실 것 좀 갖다 드릴까요?

💬 Further Expressions

- 방문객을 환영하는 표현: A에 방문하신 것을 환영합니다.
  - Welcome to A.
  - I am pleased to welcome you to A.
  - It is a pleasure to welcome you to A.
  - It is my great pleasure to welcome you to A.

- 만나서 반갑다는 표현: 당신을 만나서 반갑습니다.
  - It is nice to meet you in person.
  - It is great to meet you.
  - I'm delighted to meet you.
  - I'm glad to meet you
  - Nice to meet you.
  - Nice meeting you.

- 음료를 제안하는 표현: 마실 것 좀 갖다 드릴까요?
  - Can I get you something to drink?
  - Would you like something to drink?
  - How about something to drink?

🔍 PATTERN PRACTICE

Practice with a Partner

Let's practice the dialogue patterns and expressions that you have just learned with your partner.

A:

B:

A:

B:

A:

B:

EXTRA EXPRESSIONS

A: Did you have any trouble finding the way?
Did you have any <u>difficulty</u> finding the way?
Did you have any trouble <u>checking in at the reception desk</u>?

A: Please have a seat.
Sit down, please
Take a seat, please
Would you like to take a seat?

🔍 PRACTICE BY YOURSELF

1. Vocabulary Check-up

Match the words with the correct definition.

1. look forward to something •   • **A** personally

2. in person •   • **B** greet visitors in a friendly way when they arrive

3. welcome •   • **C** the place where people's appointments and questions are dealt with

4. reception •   • **D** feel excited about something that is going to happen because you expect to enjoy it

5. hardly •   • **E** a narrow margin by which performance was, is, or will be achieved

Complete the sentences with a the proper word. Change the form if needed.

1. Apply _____ from 9-11a.m. Weekdays.

2. It is a great pleasure to _____ you to our home.

3. Mary _____ a meeting with you as soon as possible.

4. Juan was so angry that he could _____ contain himself.

5. You can leave a message at the _____ desk if you arrive early.

2. Sentence Paraphrasing

> Practice some other sentences out loud keeping the same meaning as the given sentence.

❶ Welcome to Moontech.

❷ It is nice to meet you in person.

❸ Did you have any trouble finding the way?

Culture Tips on Welcoming Business Visitors

1. *Visitor's name and right pronunciation:* You need to ensure that you can correctly pronounce the visitor's name; even in cases of unique pronunciations. It is impolite to say a name inaccurately or use the wrong name. Therefore, it's better to ask for the visitor's name and note the pronunciation from the start.

2. *Business cards:* Business cards are not normally exchanged upon meeting. If you need a colleague's contact information, it is ok to ask them for their card. It is also okay to offer someone your card. But there is not an elaborate ritual of exchanging cards as in other cultures.

MAKE MY OWN DIALOGUE

Idea Bank

Write down what you usually do in advance to welcome visitors, how to start a conversation, and how to keep the conversation.

1. When receiving customers at your workplace, what kinds of things do you need to do in advance?

- make a reservation for the meeting room and check the Internet connection
- notify the reception about the customer visit
- confirm the meeting place with the customer

2. How do you usually start your conversations with visitors?

- talking about weather
- talking about current issues

3. What happens when a visitor arrives with an appointment to visit your company?

- meet the visitor at the reception desk
- go to the meeting room
- offer some drinks/refreshments
- start small talk

Class Discussion

Discuss the places where we usually welcome visitors. If there are more ideas or students come up with other ideas, you can add them to the list.

(Explain what kind of occasions would be at the places below.)

1. airport
2. hotel lobby
3. company reception
4. _____

Discuss the types of visitors.

1. purchaser (buyer, customer)
2. shareholders, stakeholders
3. investors
4. _____

Discuss the purpose of visiting

1. to discuss the new product development specifications
2. to sign a contract
3. to examine the company status
4. _____

My Own Dialogue

Choose one place where you welcome the visitors:
_____

Choose a type of visitor:
_____

Choose a purpose for the visit:
_____

Choose a topic to start your small talk:
_____

Based on the above selections, make your own dialogue.

A:

B:

A:

B:

A:

B:

Act Out

Act out your own dialogue in front of the class. You can get help from your partner if you need a dialogue partner.

Teacher's Model Dialogue

Mr. Blanks is a potential investor for Moontech. Before making investments at Moontech, he wants to visit the company to look around in depth. It's his first time visiting Korea and, of course, his first time visiting the company. Let's go over the dialogue held between them. Ms. Placid, a member of IR team at Moontech, welcomes him at the airport.

A: (seeing Ms. Placid holding the name card) You must be Ms. Placid.

B: Yes, I am. It is my great pleasure to welcome you to Korea.

A: Thank you. I have been looking forward to this visit. I'm also glad to meet you. We've talked quite a bit over the phone and through emails, but it's great to finally meet you in person.

B: I'm delighted to meet you, too. So how was your flight?

A: There was turbulence that kept me awake the whole time.

B: Oh, you must be tired. Why don't you go to the hotel first and get some rest?
As our schedule is planned to start from tomorrow morning, I think it would be better for you to relax.

A: Okay, that sounds good. I would like to read through the company brochure and the annual reports from last year before visiting your company tomorrow.

Chapter 13: Meeting

Issues & Schedules

At the workplace, you participate in meetings and therefore need to know how to start and conduct meetings. Let's learn how we start and manage meetings in English.

📷 SNAPSHOT

Let's learn key vocabulary/phrases you would use in a meeting situation.

agenda	schedule	conference room	bored	productive
clock	fiscal year	discussion	strategy	marathon meeting

_____   _____

_____   _____

🔎 TODAY'S SITUATION

The staff members get together and a budget meeting is about to start. They talk about the meeting agenda and management. Let's learn the sentence patterns and key expressions.

A: Let's start the budget meeting. When do you expect Linda to arrive?

B: She has just gone to make a quick phone call. She will be right back.

A: Okay, then, what is the first agenda item for today's meeting?

B: The agenda we will deal with today is to outline key budget goals for the 2015-2016 fiscal years and discuss long-term cost-cutting measures.

A: What do you think about allocating time for each topic in advance?

B: Sounds great! That will make the meeting more efficient!

✎ Check Point

- 부재중인 상대가 언제 돌아오는지에 대해 묻는 표현: **When do you expect A to arrive?**
  A가 언제 돌아올 것 같습니까?

- 회의 안건을 묻는 표현: **What is the agenda item?**
  회의 안건은 무엇입니까?

- 의견을 묻는 표현: **What do you think about A?**
  당신은 A에 대해 어떻게 생각합니까?

- 찬성하는 표현: **Sounds great.**
  좋습니다. 동의합니다.

💬 Further Expressions

- 부재중인 상대가 언제 돌아오는지에 대해 묻는 표현: A가 언제 돌아올 것 같습니까?
  - When do you expect A to arrive?
  - When will A arrive?

- 곧 돌아온다고 대답하는 표현: 곧 돌아올 것입니다.
  - She will be right back.
  - She'll return soon
  - She'll probably be back shortly.
  - She will be back in a moment.
  - It will not be long until she comes back.

- 찬성하는 표현: 좋습니다. 동의합니다.
  - (That) sounds great.
  - Terrific. / Great. / Brilliant. / Excellent. / Fabulous.
  - I agree with your opinion.
  - I agree with your idea.

🔍 PATTERN PRACTICE

Practice with a Partner

Let's practice the dialogue patterns and expressions that you have just learned with your partner.

A:

B:

A:

B:

A:

B:

EXTRA EXPRESSIONS

A: Let's start the budget meeting.
Let's <u>do</u> the work first.
<u>How/What about starting</u> the budget meeting?
<u>Shall we start</u> the budget meeting?
<u>Why don't we start</u> the budget meeting?

B: She just has gone to <u>make a quick phone call</u>.
She just has gone to <u>answer the phone</u>.
She just has gone to <u>receive a fax</u>.
She just has gone to <u>send a fax</u>.

PRACTICE BY YOURSELF

1. Vocabulary Check-up

Match the words with the correct definition.

① agenda • • Ⓐ points to be discussed at a meeting;

② conference • • Ⓑ a period used for calculating annual financial statements in businesses and other organizations

③ fiscal year • • Ⓒ reducing expenses and improving profitability

④ cost-cutting • • Ⓓ a meeting at which formal discussions take place

⑤ allocate • • Ⓔ to assign or allot for a particular purpose

Complete the sentences with a the proper word. Change the form if needed.

① The first thing on the _____ is our poor marketing results.

② The problem lies in how to _____ the expenses and how to come up with the money required.

③ Mr. Lee met many old colleagues at the marketing _____.

④ No purchases will be allowed during this year due to _____ initiatives.

⑤ The budget for the current _____ was given the final approval yesterday.

2. Sentence Paraphrasing

> Practice some other sentences out loud keeping the same meaning with the given sentence.

❶ David will be right back.

❷ I agree with your idea.

❸ Let's start the budget meeting.

Culture Tips on Meeting

1. *Importance of Time :* People from a culture where time is more flexible might believe that the meeting should end when everything has been discussed. But Americans feel differently, and they put an emphasis on rigid time schedules. When you enter a meeting with Americans, expect to see an agenda, and if you are leading the meeting, do your best to stick to the agenda. Being on time to the meeting is considered very important.

2. *Purpose of Meetings :* After a few pleasantries in the meeting room, the common term that Americans or Western people use is "Let's get down to business." Western meetings generally run on a tight schedule with an organized, pre-planned agenda. Meetings are for business. On the other hand, different cultures see the meeting as the arena for building personal relationships and strengthening bonds. Getting down to business comes further down the priority list.

MAKE MY OWN DIALOGUE

Idea Bank

What do you do before/while/after attending a meeting?

1. What kind of things do you do before a meeting?

- Go over the agenda
- Read through the related documents
- Take notes on things to discuss

---

2. What kind of things do you do during a meeting?

- Listen to others
- Respect other views
- Present opinions (agree to someone's opinions or disagree politely)

---

3. What kind of things do you do after a meeting?

- Check the minutes
- Plan how to execute action plans

Class Discussion

What kind of meetings do you usually attend? If there are more ideas or students come up with other ideas, you can add them to the list.

1. Brainstorming/board /troubleshooting/briefing
2. Informal/formal/team
3. _____

What is your role in the meeting? And what are the responsibilities?

1. A chair: outlines the agenda, states procedures, encourages people to speak
2. A participant: proposes ideas, asks questions, builds decisions
3. A facilitator: actively participates and guides the group towards consensus
4. A secretary/assistant: writes minutes/circulates them
5. _____

Discuss the meeting process flow.

1. Starting: Create a welcoming environment, review the agenda and roles
2. Cover one agenda item at a time
3. Maintain open discussion
4. Summarize decisions and agree on action items

My Own Dialogue

Choose a meeting to participate in:
_____

Choose your role:
_____

Choose the agenda to be handled:
_____

Based on the above selections, make your own dialogue.

A:

B:

A:

B:

A:

B:

Act Out

Act out your own dialogue in front of the class. You can get help from your partner if you need a dialogue partner.

Teacher's Model Dialogue

Mr. Robinson, a manager in a technical assistance team, holds an urgent technical problem solving meeting. Ms. Placid attends the meeting.

A: Ms. Placid. We will be starting our meeting in few minutes. Sorry to call you up so urgently.

B: No problem. I also thought this matter should be handled in a prompt manner.

A: OK, shall we start? Welcome, everybody, and our objective today is to solve the technical problem that occurred in our software system, Callanumber. Sam will be taking the minutes.

B: As I mentioned in the email, our client has complained the Callanumber system leads to crashes in their system.

A: Well, I guess the problem was caused by the system failure. We need to call the engineer who developed the program. Who's in charge of the program?

B: Well, Mr. Blunt is the head of the Callanumber system development team, but I'm afraid that he cannot be with us today because he has another meeting right now.

A: I see. Then I'll contact Mr. Blunt to discuss the problem, and Ms. Placid, why don't you contact the client and notify them that we are in the process of finding the cause of the problem.

B: All right.

Chapter 14

Small Talk: Topic of Interest 1

Talking about Vacations

In all workplaces, small talk is an important component in maintaining good relationships among co-workers. Therefore, you need to know how to start and continue talk on common topics such as vacations. Let's learn how we start and manage small talk in English.

📷 SNAPSHOT

Let's learn key vocabulary/phrases you can use when making small talk about vacations.

summer	surf board	palm tree	airplane ticket
reservation	taking a nap	traffic jam	a padded bill

_____   _____

_____   _____

🔍 TODAY'S SITUATION

Two colleagues are talking about their last vacation and the place they visited. Let's learn the sentence patterns and key expressions.

A: Last time we met, I remember you said you'd be taking a trip during your vacation. Where did you go?

B: I went to Hawaii with my family and enjoyed the beautiful beaches and exotic scenery.

A: Wow! It sounds great! Did you go to Waikiki beach?

B: Of course. The place was quite memorable because of the gleaming white sand, turquoise waters, and the best surf.

A: You must have had an unforgettable time with your family during your vacation.

B: Of course. I recommend that you go to Hawaii for your next vacation. I promise you won't regret it.

✏️ Check Point

- 휴가지에 대해 묻는 표현: **Where did you go for your vacation?**
  휴가로 어디를 다녀왔습니까?

- 방문 여부를 묻는 표현: **Did you go to A?**
  A에 갔습니까?

- 휴가장소의 기억에 남는 특징에 대해 말하는 표현:
  The place was quite memorable because of A.
  그 장소는 A때문에 꽤 기억에 남습니다.

- 과거 사실에 관한 강한 확신을 나타내는 표현: : **must have p.p.**
  −했었음이 틀림없습니다.

- 상대방에게 무언가를 해보라고 추천하는 표현: **I recommend you to A.**
  −저는 당신이 A를 할 것을 추천합니다.

💬 Further Expressions

- 다양한 휴가 상황에 따른 휴가 장소에 관해 질문하는 표현: 휴가로 어디를 다녀왔습니까?
  - Where did you go for your vacation?
  - Where did you go for your last vacation?
  - Where did you go for your best vacation?
  - Where did you go for your summer vacation?

- 상대방에게 무언가를 해보라고 추천하는 표현: 저는 당신이 A를 할 것을 추천합니다.
  - I recommend you to A.
  - I recommend that you A.
  - I suggest you to A.
  - I suggest that you A.

- 강한 확신을 나타내는 표현: 절대 후회하지 않는다고 제가 보장합니다.
  - I promise you won't regret it.
  - I promise.
  - I guarantee it.

🔍 PATTERN PRACTICE

Practice with a Partner

Let's practice the dialogue patterns and expressions that you have just learned with your partner.

A:

B:

A:

B:

A:

B:

EXTRA EXPRESSIONS

B: The place was quite memorable because of the gleaming white sand.
The place was quite <u>unforgettable/impressive</u> because of the gleaming white sands.
The place was quite memorable <u>because of the scenery</u>.

B: Of course
Sure.
Yes.
Certainly.
Definitely.
Why not?

🔎 PRACTICE BY YOURSELF

1. Vocabulary Check-up

Match the words with the correct definition.

① small talk

② pad the bill

③ exotic

④ gleam

⑤ turquoise

Ⓐ sparkle or shine

Ⓑ put unnecessary or additional items on a bill to make the total cost higher

Ⓒ unusual and interesting, usually because it comes from or is related to abroad

Ⓓ to be of a light, greenish-blue color

Ⓔ polite conversation (usually between people that do not know each other very well) about unimportant or uncontroversial matters, especially done on social occasions.

Complete the sentences below with the proper word. Change the form if needed.

① The topic of _____ may seem unimportant, but this is actually very important in the office.

② The glass _____ with a bright reflection.

③ I enjoyed the clear _____ sea all the time during my last summer vacation.

④ The plumber had _____ with things we didn't need.

⑤ The dish has a mysterious and _____ taste.

2. Sentence Paraphrasing

> Practice some other sentences out loud keeping the same meaning with the given sentence.

❶ Where did you go for your vacation?

❷ I recommend you to go to Hawaii for your next vacation.

❸ I promise you won't regret it.

Culture Tips on Vacations

1. ***Americans vs. Europeans:*** Europeans take almost a month of vacation in a year. Why do Europeans and Americans differ so much in their attitude toward work and leisure? Americans value stuff more than they value leisure time.

2. ***Why Americans do not travel abroad:*** According to an article in CNN, only 30 % of American citizens have passports. Tourism experts and avid travelers attribute Americans' lack of interest in international travel to a few key factors, including: the United States' own rich cultural and geographic diversity, an American skepticism and/or ignorance about international destinations, a work culture that prevents Americans from taking long vacations abroad, and the prohibitive cost and logistics of going overseas.

MAKE MY OWN DIALOGUE

Idea Bank

Share your unforgettable vacation memory.

Answer the following questions to prepare your unforgettable vacation story.

1. When was it?

   _____

2. Where did you go?

   _____

3. How did you get there?

   _____

4. What happened? What was the place like? What did you see? Was it a good/bad event?

   _____

5. Why do you think it is memorable?

   _____

Class Discussion

Where do you usually go or where would you like to go on vacation? If there are more ideas or students come up with other ideas, you can add them to the list.

1. Abroad (foreign countries)
2. To the coast and do water sports
3. To the mountains and enjoy hiking
4. _____

What's your favorite type of vacation?

1. Going to an all-inclusive resort
2. Renting an ocean-front condo
3. Going on a cruise
   _____

What do you value most when planning your vacation?

1. Lots of sightseeing
2. Playing and doing outdoor sports
3. Shopping
4. enjoying gourmet food /relaxation/ staycation
   _____

My Own Dialogue

Choose a person whom you are talking to:

_____

Choose an occasion in a business setting to talk about your vacation:

_____

Based on the above selections, make your own dialogue.

A:

B:

A:

B:

A:

B:

Act Out

Act out your own dialogue in front of the class. You can get help from your partner if you need a dialogue partner.

Teacher's Model Dialogue

Mr. Blanks and Ms. Placid are making small talk during the session break in a Global Marketing Conference.

A: Mr. Blanks, when are you planning to take your vacation this year? I remember you had a long vacation last year and travelled several countries in Europe.

B: Yeah, it was terrific. The castle hotel where we stayed in France was fantastic not only in the architecture but also the food and wines served. Anyway, we can't afford to travel abroad this year since we went over our budget on the last trip. This year, I'm just planning to go camping at the end of July.

A: Do you rent a cabin then?

B: No, we will camp in a tent. We will barbecue and spend most of the time hiking in the mountains. What about you, Ms. Placid?

A: Well, I am not an adventurer like you, so I usually spend my vacation relaxing and going to spas. This year, it's my 10th wedding anniversary, so my husband made reservations at a luxurious all-inclusive resort. I can't wait for my vacation.

Chapter 15

Small Talk: Topic of Interest 2

Talking about Health & Lifestyle

Everyone has an interest in health and healthy lifestyles, so you need to know how to start and continue talk on these common topics. Let's learn how we start and manage small talk about health and lifestyle in English.

📷 SNAPSHOT

Let's learn key vocabulary/phrases you would use when making small talk about health and lifestyle.

exercise	sound sleep	do anything regularly	waste money and effort
healthy diet	junk food	treadmill	weight training
personal training			

_____   _____
_____   _____

🔍 TODAY'S SITUATION

The following is a short dialogue on health and a healthy lifestyle. Let's learn the sentence patterns and key expressions.

A: Recently, I get tired and fatigued easily. What do you do to keep in shape?

B: I eat a balanced diet. I also take some vitamins because my body lacks vitamin C.

A: Do you take any supplements? If you do so, make sure you get some advice from a doctor before taking any. Supplements may not be good for your body.

B: I did think about that, so I haven't taken any. I am more into nutritious food. I also go to the gym regularly in order to do weight lifting and run on the treadmill.

A: What is it good for? Can exercising prevent our body from getting tired easily? Does exercising help us sweat more as it stimulates our hearts and lungs?

B: Of course. You know everything! Having healthy diets and regular work outs are worth trying in the long run. When you get older, it is important to be healthy and active.

✎ Check Point

- 건강을 유지하기 위해 어떤 노력을 하고 있는지 묻는 표현:
  What do you do to keep in shape? 건강을 유지하기 위해 무엇을 하십니까?

- 좋아함, 관심 있음을 나타내는 표현: **I am into A.**
  저는 A를 좋아합니다/A에 빠져있습니다.

- 목적(B)을 위하여 규칙적으로 행동(A)을 하고 있음을 나타내는 표현:
  I do A regularly in order to B. 저는 B하기 위해서 규칙적으로 A를 합니다.

- 이득을 얻는 주체에 대해 묻는 표현: **What is it good for?**
  그것은 무엇에 좋습니까?

💬 Further Expressions

- 건강을 유지하기 위해 어떤 노력을 하고 있는지 묻는 표현: 건강을 유지하기 위해 무엇을 하십니까?
  - **What do you do to keep in shape?**
  - **What do you do to keep healthy?**
  - **What do you do to stay healthy?**
  - **What do you do for your health?**

- 좋아함, 관심 있음을 나타내는 표현: 저는 A를 좋아합니다/A에 빠져있습니다.
  - **I am into A.**
  - **I am interested in A.**
  - **I am a fan of A.**
  - **I enjoy A.**

- 목적(B)을 위하여 규칙적으로 행동(A)을 하고 있음을 나타내는 표현: 저는 B하기 위해서 규칙적으로 A를 합니다.
  - **I do A regularly in order to B.**
  - **I do A regularly in order that B.**

🔍 PATTERN PRACTICE

Practice with a Partner

Let's practice the dialogue patterns and expressions that you have just learned with your partner.

A:

B:

A:

B:

A:

B:

EXTRA EXPRESSIONS

A: Make sure you get some advice from a doctor before taking any.
Make certain you get some advice from doctors before taking any.
You should get some advice from doctors before taking any.
Ensure that you get some advice from doctors before taking any.

A: Can exercising prevent our body from getting tired easily?
Can exercising keep our body from getting tired easily?
Can exercising prevent us from gaining weight?

PRACTICE BY YOURSELF

1. Vocabulary Check-up

Match the words with the correct definition.

1. fatigued • • **A** suffering from extreme physical or mental tiredness

2. supplement • • **B** take part in physical exercise, as in training

3. treadmill • • **C** over or after a long period of time; in the end

4. work out • • **D** a pill that you take or a special kind of food that you eat in order to improve your health

5. in the long run • • **E** a piece of equipment, for example an exercise machine, consisting of a continuous moving belt

Complete the sentences below with the proper word. Change the form if needed.

1. I bought a multiple vitamin and mineral _____ for my father's birthday present.

2. My insomnia has left me feeling extremely _____. I frequently ache all over because of lack of sleep.

3. In order to stay healthy, I _____ regularly and never eat to excess.

4. _____, you should exercise to relieve your stress completely.

5. The expensive _____ I bought for exercising has been collecting dust.

2. Sentence Paraphrasing

Practice some other sentences out loud keeping the same meaning with the given sentence.

❶ What do you do to keep in shape?

❷ I am into A.

❸ Make sure you get some advice from a doctor before taking any.

Culture Tips on Health & Lifestyle

1. *Advising on health:* Koreans give others advice on health often, especially on what they should eat and how they should keep in shape or keep the body healthy. In Western culture, it's the individual's responsibility and considered to be a private issue.

2. *Green office:* As people are developing more interest in an eco-friendly environment, Britain started "Green Office Week" in 2009 to encourage workers across the UK to make small changes to their working habits to positively impact the environment. The week raises awareness of key green issues, providing office workers with the practical advice, tools, and help they need to create a more sustainable way of working.

 MAKE MY OWN DIALOGUE

Idea Bank

Share your memories on health and your lifestyle.

1. Talk about an incident when you were very sick or had an injury.

1. When was it?

   _____

2. How did it happen?

   _____

3. What did you do to overcome it?

   _____

4. What did you learn from the incident?

   _____

2. What kind of lifestyle do you maintain?

- "Early Bird" /"Night Owl" type
- Income or occupation based lifestyles/life based on religious preferences
- Activism/Simple living

_____

Class Discussion

What kind of sickness do you suffer from often? If there are more ideas or students come up with other ideas, you can add them to the list.

1. cold/flu
2. stomachache, headache
3. food poisoning, asthma
4. _____

What kind of injuries have you experienced in your life?

1. cut finger, burnt my hand, have a bruise, scratch
2. twist my ankle, break my leg,
3. concussion, knock myself unconscious

_____

What do you do to maintain your health?

1. Healthy eating
2. Regular physical activity (jogging, running, cycling, etc.)
3. Keeping a healthy mind (reducing stress)
4. Not taking harmful drugs or alcohol
5. Practice safe living habits
6. Get regular health care

_____

My Own Dialogue

Choose a person whom you are talking to:

_____

Choose an occasion in a business setting to talk about health or lifestyle:

_____

Based on the above selections, make your own dialogue.

A:

B:

A:

B:

A:

B:

Act Out

Act out your own dialogue in front of the class. You can get help from your partner if you need a dialogue partner.

Teacher's Model Dialogue

Ms. Placid meets Mr. Robinson as they are going into a meeting.

A: Mr. Robinson, long time no see! I heard that you were on sick leave.

B: Yes, I broke my leg, so I could not walk for weeks. Since I couldn't drive with the broken leg, I decided to take the leave.

A: You must have suffered a lot. Did you have an accident?

B: You know that I really enjoy cycling. I was cycling at night, and there was another bike that was coming from the other direction. But we could not see each other, so we crashed into each other.

A: Are you okay now?

B: I had a cast for a month, but I feel much better now. From the incident, I decided to keep safe living habits that I did not consider important. I was too confident about my cycling skills and did not put the cycling lights on, and that caused a big problem.

A: Well, you learned a lesson from it though. People shut the stable door after the horse has bolted. Hope you get well soon!

Chapter 16

Small Talk: Topic of Interest 3

Talking about Social Networking

These days, people communicate by social networks and have conversations about social networking among colleagues. Let's learn how we start and manage small talk about social networking in English.

📷 SNAPSHOT

Let's learn key vocabulary/phrases you would use when making small talk about social networking.

Facebook	Twitter	followers	blue	celebrity
on the web	smart phone	iPod	iPhone	cyber bullying
Mark Zukerberg				

_____   _____

_____   _____

🔍 TODAY'S SITUATION

The following is a short dialogue on social networking. Let's learn the sentence patterns and key expressions.

A: I've registered and started using Facebook. You can get in touch with me by Facebook now.

B: Wow, congratulations. Welcome to the new world. But it's amazing you didn't make a Facebook account until recently.

A: Actually, I had joined before, but I made the account again a few days ago. I found out the advantage of social networking is connecting colleagues on the web as well as in reality.

B: But some people insist that social networking or user-generated content affects one's life too much. For example, they don't get enough personal space in their own life.

A: I saw the content you posted on your Twitter and retweeted it to my twitter followers.

B: I've gained 57 more followers thanks to your retweeting.

✎ Check Point

- 통신수단을 통해 연락할 수 있음을 나타내는 표현:
  You can get in touch with me by A 당신은 A라는 수단을 통해 나와 연락할 수 있습니다.

- 놀라움을 나타내는 표현: **It's amazing (that)~**
  ~라니 놀랍군요.

- 장점을 나타내는 표현: **The advantage of A is B.**
  A의 장점은 B입니다.

- 다른 사람들의 주장을 나타내는 표현: **Some people insist (that) ~**
  어떤 사람들은 ~라고 주장합니다.

- 소셜 네트워크 B에 게시한 A 내용 혹은 글을 보았음을 나타내는 표현:
  I saw A you posted on B. 저는 당신이 B에 게시한 A를 보았습니다.

💬 Further Expressions

- 통신수단을 통해 연락할 수 있음을 나타내는 표현: 당신은 A라는 수단을 통해 나와 연락할 수 있습니다.
  - **You can get in touch with me by/through A.**
  - **You can contact me by/through A.**
  - **You can make contact with me by/through A.**
  - **You can communicate with me by/through A.**

- 다른 사람들의 주장을 나타내는 표현: 어떤 사람들은 A라고 주장합니다.
  - **Some people insist (that) ~**
  - **They argue/claim/assert/maintain (that) ~**

- 소셜 네트워크 B에 게시한 A 내용 혹은 글을 보았음을 나타내는 표현: 저는 당신이 B에 게시한 A를 보았습니다.
  - **I saw A you posted on B.**
  - **I read your (A) posting on B.**

🔎 PATTERN PRACTICE

Practice with a Partner

Let's practice the dialogue patterns and expressions that you have just learned with your partner.

A:

B:

A:

B:

A:

B:

EXTRA EXPRESSIONS

B: It's amazing you didn't make a Facebook account until recently.

It's astonishing/incredible/shocking that you didn't make a Facebook account until recently.

You are amazing not to have made a Facebook account until recently.

B: I've gained 57 more followers thanks to your retweeting.

I've gained 57 more followers due to/because of your retweeting.

I've gained 57 more followers thanks to the effort.

🔍 PRACTICE BY YOURSELF

1. Vocabulary Check-up

Match the words with the correct definition.

① register

② tweet

③ user-generated content

④ get in touch

⑤ cyber bullying

Ⓐ actions that use information and communication technologies to support deliberate, repeated, and hostile behavior by an individual or group that is intended to harm another or others

Ⓑ make contact and communicate

Ⓒ a message sent using Twitter

Ⓓ material on websites produced by the users of the website

Ⓔ put a name on an official list in order to be able to do the thing or to receive a service

Complete the sentences below with the proper word. Change the form if needed.

① _____ is a major issue for sites like Facebook and Kakao Talk.

② _____ with me as soon as you make your account on Facebook.

③ I do my _____ with my friends anytime, anywhere.

④ Hundreds lined up to _____ to vote.

⑤ Major companies took notice of the popularity of _____ and its commercial potential.

2. Sentence Paraphrasing

> Practice some other sentences out loud keeping the same meaning with the given sentence.

① You can get in touch with me by A.

② Some people insist that social networking affects one's life too much.

③ It's amazing you didn't make a Facebook account until recently.

Culture Tips on Social Networking

1. *Posting pictures on the web:* In North America and the UK, most people don't hesitate to share photos of themselves on their profile. Korean and Japanese users are uncomfortable with posting pictures of themselves on their personal intranet pages, preferring to use avatars or pictures of pets.

2. *Professional social networking platform:* In Korea, it is still considered to be polite to give business cards to the person that you first meet. But nowadays, Westerners think it's outdated, and they prefer to exchange their social networking information. For example, "LinkedIn" is a business oriented social networking service and represents real-world professional relationships.

MAKE MY OWN DIALOGUE

Idea Bank

Which social networks do you use and why?

1. Why do you use social networks?

- to keep in touch with people and expand my business network
- to gather information
- to keep my individuality

2. Think about your social networks in the past and present.

- Which social network did you use most in the past and why?

- Which social network do you use most now and why?

Class Discussion

Which social networking sites/tools have you heard of? Which have you used? Which would you recommend?

1. Facebook/MySpace/Twitter/LinkedIn
2. online cafés/blogs
3. _____

Do you see social networking as something you do for work or for pleasure? What can you do to get the most out of social networking for work?

1. Anyone whose job involves networking and socializing can benefit from spending time building and maintaining a professional social network.
2. To make your social network work actively, you need to set aside some time every day to build and maintain your network. Also, you need to make the effort to stay in touch with people and make sure you always reply to their messages.

_____

What kind of phrases do you use for social networking?

1. Thanks for the follow.
2. Thanks for the RT.
3. Great post!
4. Great link!

_____

My Own Dialogue

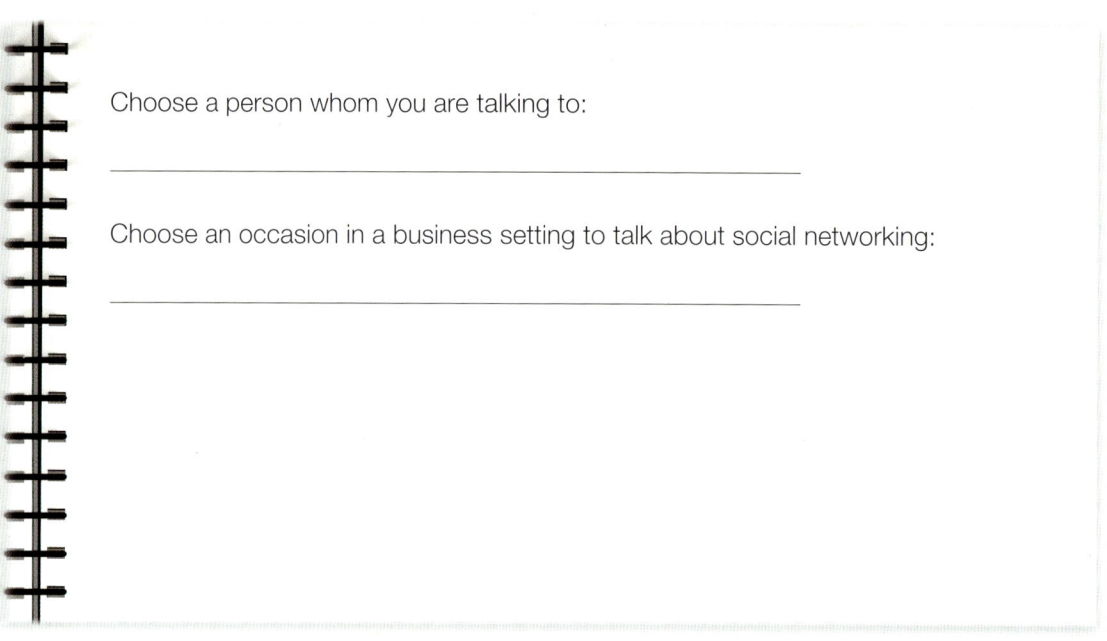

Choose a person whom you are talking to:

_____

Choose an occasion in a business setting to talk about social networking:

_____

Based on the above selections, make your own dialogue.

A:

B:

A:

B:

A:

B:

Act Out

Act out your own dialogue in front of the class. You can get help from your partner if you need a dialogue partner.

Teacher's Model Dialogue

Ms. Placid meets Mr. Robinson as they are going into a meeting.

A: Mr. Robinson, how have you been? I loved that article you shared on Facebook about the habits of successful people.

B: Oh, yes, I also thought it was very interesting. I didn't know that you had a Facebook account. Why did you wait so long to friend me?

A: Actually, I temporarily shut down my account for the past few months. Sometimes I feel like I can't concentrate on my work or personal life as much when my account is active.

B: I know what you mean. My wife is always on Facebook or Twitter posting photos and sharing videos. I mainly use social networking to keep up with current events and stay in touch with friends and family.

A: Yeah, thanks for accepting my friend request. I didn't realize we have many of the same hobbies until I saw your Facebook profile. I look forward to the future posts you share!

Chapter 17

Arrangements

Getting Together

In business situations, you have to make, accept, and decline invitations from your coworkers. Therefore, you need to know how to deal with these situations with appropriate and natural expressions. Let's learn how we manage invitation situations in English.

📷 SNAPSHOT

Let's learn key vocabulary/phrases you would use when making, accepting, or declining invitations.

invitation card	valid refusal reasons	birthday party	business party
present	dinner	schedule	get-together
make a reservation			
_____	_____		
_____	_____		

🔍 TODAY'S SITUATION

There is a short dialogue on making and accepting an invitation. Let's learn the sentence patterns and key expressions.

A: Do you remember Diana? She is a paralegal in my company. I'd like to invite you to go with me to Diana's birthday party next Sunday.

B: Of course, I remember her. She had a beautiful smile. Thank you, I'd love to. What time is the party?

A: The party is at 7:00 p.m., so I will pick you up at 6:30.

B: Thank you. I was wondering if you could bring a present for her. I am not quite sure what kind of present she would like.

A: I think the best present is what the receiver needs or wants. Let me check what she needs or wants, and after that we can go together to buy it.

B: That's a good idea. I'd be delighted that you would do that for me. Thanks a lot.

A: Let me just confirm that, next Sunday, at 6:30, at your place.

✏️ Check Point

- 초대하는 표현: **I'd like to invite you to A.**
  당신을 A에 초대하고 싶습니다.

- 초대를 수락하는 표현: **Thank you, I'd love to.**
  (초대해 주셔서) 감사합니다. 참석하고 싶습니다.

- 요청, 부탁하는 표현: **I was wondering if ~**
  ~해 주실 수 있는지 궁금합니다.

- 자신이 행동할 것임을 나타내는 표현: **Let me check (that) ~**
  제가 ~을 확인해볼게요.

- 약속을 확실히 하는 표현: **Let me confirm (that) ~**
  ~로 확정합니다.

💬 Further Expressions

- 초대하는 표현: 당신을 A에 초대하고 싶습니다.
  - I'd like to invite you to A.
  - I would like to ask you to come to A.
  - I was wondering if I could invite you to A.
  - It would be my pleasure if you come to A.
  - May I have the honor of your presence at A?

- 초대를 수락하는 표현: (초대해 주셔서) 감사합니다. 참석하고 싶습니다.
  - Thank you, I'd love to.
  - Thank you for your invitation.
  - Of course, that would be great.
  - Sure, I will go.
  - I'd be delighted.

- 초대를 거절하는 표현: 죄송하지만, 초대에 응하지 못합니다.
  - I'm afraid I can't. I have other plans.
  - I'm terribly sorry, but I can't.
  - Thank you for asking, but I'm busy.
  - I'd love to, but I can't.
  - Sounds good, but I don't think I can. I have to work late.

🔍 PATTERN PRACTICE

Practice with a Partner

Let's practice the dialogue patterns and expressions that you have just learned with your partner.

A:

B:

A:

B:

A:

B:

EXTRA EXPRESSIONS

B: I was wondering if you could bring a present for her.
I was wondering if you could come along.
I was wondering if you would accept my proposal.
I was wondering if you had time.

A: Let me confirm what she needs or wants.
Let me confirm that they are coming.
Let me check the reasons why David accepted the proposal.

PRACTICE BY YOURSELF

1. Vocabulary Check-up

Match the words with the correct definition.

1. paralegal
2. delighted
3. honor
4. get together
5. confirm

A. extremely pleased and excited
B. something special and desirable
C. to meet with somebody for social purposes or to discuss or organize something
D. a professional who has the ability to perform substantive legal work
E. to show that something is definitely true

Complete the sentences with the proper word. Change the form if needed.

1. Ellis is the new _____ helping my boss.

2. Ellen was now satisfied that the family _____ had been restored.

3. I am writing to _____ a booking for a single room for the night of June 7th.

4. Jonathan was _____ that his only son was well again after operation.

5. We must _____ for a drink some time.

2. Sentence Paraphrasing

> Practice some other sentences out loud keeping the same meaning with the given sentence.

① I'd like to invite you to A.

② Thank you for your invitation.

③ I'm afraid I can't go.

Culture Tips on Invitation

1. ***Replying to an Invitation:*** When you get a formal invitation, the invitation cards or similar document is often marked with "R.S.V.P." It is standard practice to reply to an RSVP request whether confirming attendance or declining. It does not mean to respond only if you're coming. It means the host needs a definite head count for the planned event and needs it by the date specified on the invitation. Americans need certainty, so saying, "I will try to come" may make most Americans feel uncomfortable. Also, reasons for not attending should be stated to be polite. If you receive a written invitation that says RSVP, make sure you respond by letter, email, or phone, telling the host whether or not you will be attending.

2. ***Goodbye Messages:*** "See you later", "Drop by sometime", or "Let's get together sometime" are often meant as a friendly goodbye rather than an actual invitation. When in doubt, do not be too shy to clarify whether it's an invitation or not.

MAKE MY OWN DIALOGUE

Idea Bank

Do you like to get together with your business colleagues?

1. What kind of get-togethers do you have after work?

- What kind? _____

- Who attends? _____

- Where do you go? _____

- What kind of conversations are held?

_____

2. Have you ever been invited to a get-together from a business associate?

- When? _____

- What kind? _____

- Did you accept or decline? Why?

_____

Class Discussion

What kind of get-togethers are there? Is each formal or informal? If there are more ideas or students come up with other ideas, you can add them to the list.

1. Yes: It could be a good chance to get to know others better. Through get-togethers, you can have more intimacy.
2. No: I do not want to spend my private time seeing the people who are related with my work.

_____

How could you decline invitations graciously? What kind of phrases would you use?

1. Express appreciation for the invitation.
2. Express regret that you must decline. Your regret sounds more sincere if you can give a specific explanation of what prevents your acceptance.

_____

My Own Dialogue

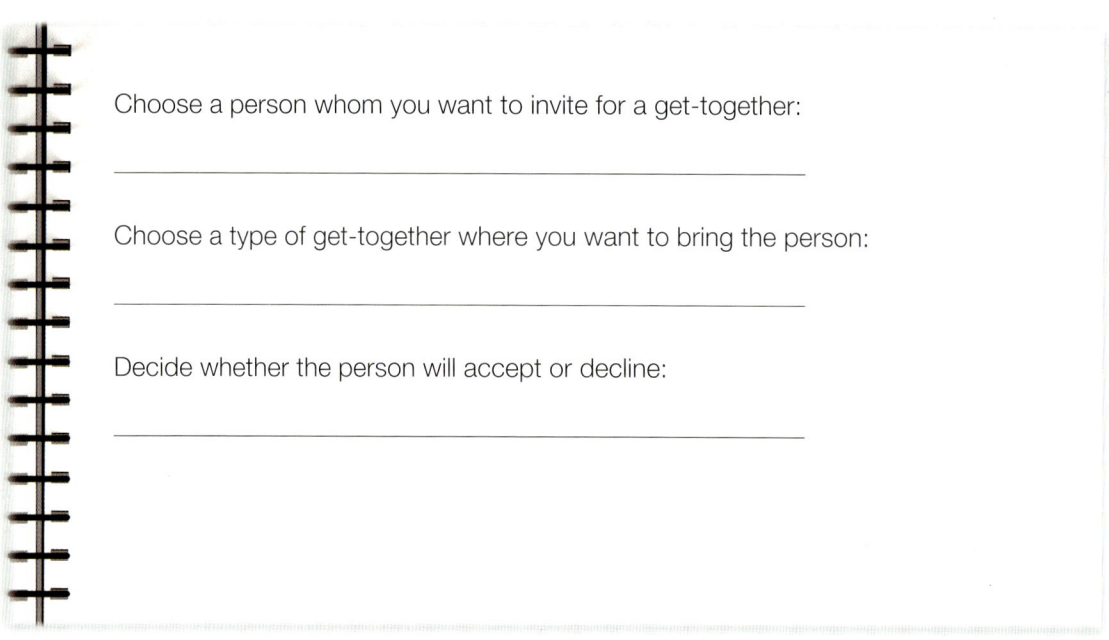

Choose a person whom you want to invite for a get-together:

_____

Choose a type of get-together where you want to bring the person:

_____

Decide whether the person will accept or decline:

_____

💬 **Based on the above selections, make your own dialogue.**

A:

B:

A:

B:

A:

B:

Act Out

Act out your own dialogue in front of the class. You can get help from your partner if you need a dialogue partner.

Teacher's Model Dialogue

Act out your own dialogue in front of the class. You can get help from your partner if you need a dialogue partner.

A: Mr. Blanks, do you have any plans today? Every Friday after work, our team members go out for Happy Hour. I was wondering if you'd like to join us this evening.

B: That would be nice. Thank you.

A: Happy Hour starts at 5, and we will leave our office a little early. Say 4:50?

B: Oh, then I'll have to arrange the meeting with the technical support team a little earlier so I can make it in time. Where exactly do you go, and how many people will be going?

A: There will just be the six of us, and we will go to the brewery pub right next to our building.

B: Could I go there directly after the meeting? Let's say between 5 and 5:30.

A: No problem. Let's confirm that we will meet at the pub around 5.

B: Great! I'm looking forward to it.

Chapter 18

Leading Conversations

Holding/Changing the Topic

In a business situation, you need to know how to hold or change topics with appropriate and valid expressions. Let's learn how we manage conversations by holding or changing subjects in English.

📷 SNAPSHOT

Let's learn key vocabulary/phrases you would use when you lead a conversation.

by the way	actually	topic	conversation partners
listening carefully	off the topic	off the record	gossip
incidentally	chairman		

_____   _____

_____   _____

🔍 TODAY'S SITUATION

The following is a short dialogue in a business meeting. Examine carefully how the participants hold and change topics with appropriate signal words. Let's learn the sentence patterns and key expressions.

A: I think that's all we need to talk about regarding this month's report. Let's turn to next month's report, shall we? I didn't get a copy of it. Could someone hand me one?

B: By the way, I have just one last comment before we move our focus to next month's report. It seems to me that we need more information on how the sales department is doing.

A: That's a good point. Actually, I wanted to ask you for more information regarding the sales department's achievements to be included in next month's report.

B: I'm sure I can get the information from Ms. Lee. Oh, incidentally, that reminds me the fact that Ms. Lee is quitting, and Ms. Park will be taking her place. This is off the record, of course.

A: While we're on the subject of personnel changes, did you know that Ms. Park is being promoted to sales manager next month?

B: I hadn't heard that, but I'm not surprised. She's been in line for that job for years. Anyway, we need to get back to next month's report.

✏️ **Check Point**

- 화제를 전환하는 표현: **by the way; incidentally; anyway**
  그런데, 그건 그렇고

- 새로운 화제에 대한 이야기를 시작하는 표현1: **I wanted to ask you about A.**
  A에 대해서 당신에게 질문하고 싶었습니다.

- 새로운 화제에 대한 이야기를 시작하는 표현2: **That reminds me A.**
  그것이 나에게 A를 떠오르게 합니다.

- 화제를 이어가며 대화를 계속하는 표현: **While we're on the subject,**
  말이 나온 김에, 그 주제에 대해 말하는 김에

💬 **Further Expressions**

- 화제를 전환하는 표현, 새로운 화제에 대한 이야기를 시작하는 표현
  - **By the way** 그런데, 그건 그렇고
  - **Incidentally** 그런데, 그건 그렇고
  - **Anyway** 게다가, 어쨌든
  - **That reminds me (of)** 그러고 보니
  - **Before I forget** 잊어버리기 전에
  - **Oh, while I remember** 잊어버리기 전에
  - **There's something else I wanted to say/ask you** 네게 물어보고 싶은 게 더 있어.

- 화제를 이어가며 대화를 계속하는 표현: 말이 나온 김에, 그 주제에 대해 말하는 김에
  - **While we're on the subject**
  - **While on the subject**

🔍 PATTERN PRACTICE

Practice with a Partner

Let's practice the dialogue patterns and expressions that you have just learned with your partner.

A:

B:

A:

B:

A:

B:

EXTRA EXPRESSIONS

A: Let's turn to next month's report, shall we?
How/What about turning to next month's report?
Why don't we turn to next month's report?
Let's go, shall we?

A: Could someone hand me one?
Could someone please hand me one?
Would someone hand me one?
Would someone please hand me one?

🔎 PRACTICE BY YOURSELF

1. Vocabulary Check-up

Match the words with the correct definition.

1. off the record • • A the people who work in a company, organization, or military force

2. personnel • • B unofficial and not supposed to be made public

3. promote • • C indicating the subject that is being talked or written about; about

4. regarding • • D to give something to someone else with your hand

5. hand • • E advancement in rank or position

Complete the sentences with the proper word. Change the form if needed.

1. This is _____, but I disagree with the manager's point of view on this matter.

2. Helen was _____ to senior manager.

3. Companies should hire and cultivate talented _____.

4. Laura _____ her teacher a slip of paper.

5. _____ your recent inquiry, I have enclosed a copy of our new leaflet.

2. Sentence Paraphrasing

> Practice some other sentences out loud keeping the same meaning with the given sentence.

❶ Oh, incidentally, that reminds me of the fact that Ms. Lee is quitting.

❷ Let's turn to next month's report, shall we?

❸ Could someone hand me one?

Culture Tips on Communication

1. *High-context cultures:* Asians, Latin Americans, and Middle Easterners have high-context cultures. They infer information from message context, rather than from content. They prefer indirectness, politeness, and ambiguity. They convey little information explicitly and rely heavily on nonverbal signs.

2. *Low-context cultures:* Europeans, Scandinavians, North Americans have low-context cultures. They rely more on content rather than on context. They explicitly spell out information and value directness. They see indirectness as manipulative and value written word more than oral statements.

3. *Topics of conversation:* It is usually not considered polite to ask someone overly private questions such as their age, marital status, or income. Also topics like politics and religions are not suitable topic to discuss in a business setting.

# MAKE MY OWN DIALOGUE

Idea Bank

Think about a casual conversation with someone familiar. How is your usual conversation held?

1. What kind of topics do you usually talk about with someone close?

- family, relationships
- interest, business, environment, current events
- hobbies, future plans

2. Do you stay on topic? Think about a conversation that you had yesterday and write down all the topics that you talked about. Does it have any coherence?

- friend → lifestyle → social issues

Class Discussion

What is most difficult when you lead a conversation? If there are more ideas or students come up with other ideas, you can add them to the list.

1. getting off of point
2. the conversation gets too boring
3. too many pauses

_____

How do you make people stay on topic?

1. limit the time to discuss the issues
2. remind them they are side-tracked
3. announce the next topic

_____

My Own Dialogue

Choose an occasion when you are leading a conversation:
_____

Choose a topic for discussion:
_____

Choose a second topic that "B" would rather discuss:
_____

Choose a phrase that "B" will use to change the topic:
_____

Based on the above selections, make your own dialogue.

A:

B:

A:

B:

A:

B:

Act Out

Act out your own dialogue in front of the class. You can get help from your partner if you need a dialogue partner.

Teacher's Model Dialogue

Ms. Placid and Mr. Blanks are keeping the conversation on marketing issues.

A: Mr. Blanks, there is no easy way to deal with tough clients, especially the top VIPs.

B: That's why more companies are now focusing on premium marketing. We should set up a premium marketing group to find out what the customers' needs are.

A: You know sometimes they become the worst consumers though. I once handled a really bad complaint. The man was upset about the marketing promotion that we did. He was classified as one of the VIPs so I really didn't know what to do.

B: By the way, did you start the new marketing promotion?

A: No, we will be starting from next week. I need to finish up the details with the promotion event.

B: I think we are getting side-tracked. We should stick to our original topic of discussion.

A: Okay, let's get back to talking about how to organize the premium marketing teams.

Chapter 19

Dining

Business Meals / Drinks

Business meals and drinks are inevitable in Korean business circumstances. You could have a chance to get together for business meals and drinks with foreign coworkers. Let's learn how we manage conversation during these situations in English.

📷 SNAPSHOT

Let's learn key vocabulary/phrases you would use regarding business meals and drinks.

get together	work-related dinner	company dinner
propose a toast	corporate credit card	position drinks
split the bill	treat	

_____   _____

_____   _____

🔍 TODAY'S SITUATION

Davis and his colleagues are having a get-together to celebrate Davis' promotion. Let's learn the sentence patterns and key expressions regarding business meals and drinks.

A: Could I propose a toast to my colleagues to honor Davis? He was promoted to the position of Section Chief. May our company prosper, may Davis' future be filled with luck! Cheers!

B: Cheers! Thanks a million. It's awesome. Help yourself, and enjoy all you want. I'm treating you!

A: Congratulations, Davis! I envy you. Your success is amazing. You are on the fast track to becoming CEO.

B: You know I've tried my best to succeed, and with your tremendous help, I could achieve my goals and turn my dreams into reality. Thank you.

A: Don't mention it. You are indeed an incredible man. Let me tell you about the food on the menu. I'm looking forward to an excellent dinner.

B: Order whatever you want! It's on me.

✎ Check Point

- 건배/축배를 제의하는 표현: **Could I propose a toast to A?**
  A를 위해 건배/축배를 제안해도 될까요?

- 건배/축배 표현1: **May ~!**
  ~을 위하여!

- 건배/축배 표현2: **Cheers!**
  건배!

- 자신이 대접/계산할 것을 나타내는 표현: **I'm treating you. It's on me**
  내가 낼게. 내가 계산할게.

- 음식에 대해 설명을 시작하려는 표현: **Let me tell you about the food in A.**
  A에 있는 음식에 대해 설명해줄게.

💬 Further Expressions

- 건배/축배 표현2: 건배!
  - Cheers!
  - Bottoms up!
  - Down the hatch!

- 자신이 대접/계산할 것을 나타내는 표현: 내가 낼게. 내가 계산할게.
  - I'm treating you.
  - It's on me.
  - This is my treat.
  - I will treat you.
  - I'll pay for it.
  - I will take care of it.

- 각자 비용을 나눠 계산하자고 제안하는 표현: 비용을 나눠서 계산하자.
  - Let's split the bill.
  - Let's divide the cost.
  - We would like to pay separately.

🔍 PATTERN PRACTICE

Practice with a Partner

Let's practice the dialogue patterns and expressions that you have just learned with your partner.

A:

B:

A:

B:

A:

B:

EXTRA EXPRESSIONS

A: Could I propose a toast to my colleagues to honor Davis?
    I'd like to propose a toast to my colleagues to honor Davis.
    Could I make a toast to my colleagues to honor Davis?
    Could I toast Davis?

A: Don't mention it.
    You're welcome.
    My pleasure.
    No problem.
    Not at all.

PRACTICE BY YOURSELF

1. Vocabulary Check-up

Match the words with the correct definition.

1. propose a toast
2. get-together
3. help yourself
4. incredible
5. cuisine

A. an expression meaning please take whatever you want without asking permission

B. ask people to wish somebody health, happiness and success by raising their glasses and drinking

C. an informal meeting or party, usually arranged for a particular purpose

D. extremely or unusually good

E. A style or method of cooking, especially as characteristic of a particular country, region, or establishment

Complete the sentences below with the proper word. Change the form if needed.

1. I'm delighted to do the honors this evening and _____ to the bride and groom.

2. _____ to anything you like on the table.

3. Why don't we just have a small _____ next Friday?

4. I have _____ news that will surprise you.

5. The hotel is known for its excellent _____.

2. Sentence Paraphrasing

Practice some other sentences out loud keeping the same meaning with the given sentence.

① I'm treating you.

② Let's split the bill.

③ Could I propose a toast to my colleagues to honor Davis?

Culture Tips on Dining

1. ***Vegetarians:*** There are many vegetarians in other countries due to religious, ethical, environmental reasons or dietary preferences. You need to respect their preferences, so do not suggest any food containing meat. Also, remember that many Korean foods have some animal product (e.g. Kimchi has fish sauce), so when you are hosting a vegetarian, be sure not to make a mistake.

2. ***Tipping culture:*** Many visitors to the U.S. feel pressured to tip even when they do not feel it is fair or reasonable to do so. Customers cannot be forced to tip as a matter of law, but they are legally required to pay any charges that are clearly marked prior to service, and these may include mandatory gratuities (tips). In restaurant, 15% of the bill amount is considered appropriate, for porters $1~2 per bag, and hotel maids $2~3 for a night.

MAKE MY OWN DIALOGUE

Idea Bank

What are the differences between casual meals and business meals?

1. What are casual meals like with your friends and your family?

- Where do you usually go?

- What kind of foods do you eat?

- What kind of conversation go on during the casual meals?

2. What are businesses meals like with business partners?

- Where do you usually go?

- What kind of foods do you eat?

- What kind of conversation go on during the business meals?

Class Discussion

What do you need to do before taking your business partner out for a meal? If there are more ideas or students come up with other ideas, you can add them to the list.

1. ask the person's food preferences
2. check how many people will be attending
3. make reservations
4. give the telephone number or a map to the attendees

What could be things to avoid when having a meal with foreigners?

1. sitting on the floor
2. speaking with food in your mouth, chewing too loudly
3. sharing food (especially soup)
4. applying makeup after eating at the dinner table

Where would you like to take your foreign business collegue out? Why?

1. Korean traditional restaurants: To let them know more about Korean traditions
2. Korean barbecue places: Most foreigners like meat, and they are also popular eating out spots for Koreans as well
3. Western restaurants: They don't feel burdened about trying new food

My Own Dialogue

Choose a business partner to have a meal with (include nationality):
_____

Choose a place to have the meal together:
_____

Choose the kinds of food to enjoy together:
_____

Based on the above selections, make your own dialogue.

A:

B:

A:

B:

A:

B:

Act Out

Act out your own dialogue in front of the class. You can get help from your partner if you need a dialogue partner.

Teacher's Model Dialogue

Ms. Placid and Mr. Blanks are having dinner together.

A: Mr. Blanks, how are you enjoying the Korean dishes?

B: They're wonderful! I would like to get some information on this dish. It's so colorful, but I don't get how to eat this.

A: It's called "Gujeolpan" and there are nine different ingredients. What you need to do is take out one mini-pancake from the center, and put all these 9 ingredients inside, wrap it, and then eat it.

B: It is also very tasty.

A: I noticed you didn't try the meat dish. Are you a vegetarian?

B: No, but I try to avoid fatty foods, and besides, it looks spicy.

A: We should order drinks. How about some Korean drinks? Let me explain each in detail.

Chapter 20: Saying Goodbye

Business Etiquette

You need to know how to say goodbye with the appropriate expressions and etiquette in business circumstances. Let's learn how we express goodbye in English.

📷 SNAPSHOT

Let's learn key vocabulary/phrases you would use regarding saying goodbye.

goodbye	regards	fatigue	Thank you
keep in touch	email address	phone number	etiquette
resign	retirement		

_____   _____

_____   _____

🔍 TODAY'S SITUATION

Here's a situation about saying goodbye in business. Let's learn the sentence patterns and key expressions regarding saying goodbye with appropriate business etiquette.

A: It's time to wrap up the meeting. We've finished the 2 month project!

B: Awesome! Why don't we have a get-together tonight?

A: I'm afraid I have to be on my way. I have other plans with my wife. Thank you for the support and encouragement you have provided me during the collaborative project.

B: I appreciate having had the opportunity to work with you. You have a keen insight into recent business circumstances.

A: I am so flattered. Actually, I've learned a lot from you. Please keep in touch.

B: Of course. Good bye. Take care.

✎ Check Point

- 회의를 마치는 표현: **It's time to wrap up the meeting.**
  회의를 마무리할 시간이다.

- 떠나야 함을 나타내는 표현: **I'm afraid I have to be on my way.**
  죄송하지만 이만 가봐야겠어요.

- 감사함을 나타내는 표현: **Thank you for A. I appreciate A.**
  A에 대해 감사합니다.

- 계속 연락하고 지내자는 표현: **Please keep in touch.**
  계속 연락하며 지냅시다.

- 작별인사 표현: **Good bye. Take care.**
  안녕히 계세요.

💬 Further Expressions

- 떠나야 함을 나타내는 표현: 죄송하지만 이만 가야겠어요.
  - I'm afraid I have to be on my way.
  - I'm sorry, but I should be on my way
  - I'm afraid I've got to go now.
  - I'm sorry I should go now.
  - I'm sorry, but I'd better go right now.

- 계속 연락하고 지내자는 표현: 계속 연락하며 지냅시다.
  - Please keep in touch.
  - Please stay in touch.
  - Please be in touch.

- 과한 칭찬을 받았음을 나타내는 표현: 과찬이십니다.
  - I am so flattered.
  - This is very flattering.
  - You're very generous with your compliments.
  - You overpraise.
  - That is an overstatement.

🔍 PATTERN PRACTICE

Practice with a Partner

Let's practice the dialogue patterns and expressions that you have just learned with your partner.

A:

B:

A:

B:

A:

B:

EXTRA EXPRESSIONS

B: Why don't we have a get-together tonight?
Let's have a get-together tonight.
How/What about having a get-together tonight?
What do you think about having a get-together tonight?

B: Good bye.
Take care.
See you later.
Farewell.

🔍 PRACTICE BY YOURSELF

1. Vocabulary Check-up

Match the words with the correct definition.

1. regards • • A goodbye, an act of departure

2. wrap up • • B a sentiment expressing good wishes

3. farewell • • C to be grateful or thankful

4. appreciate • • D to cause (someone) to feel pleased by showing respect, affection, or admiration

5. flatter • • E to bring to a conclusion

Complete the sentences with the proper word. Change the form if needed.

1. Give my _____ to Anne.

2. Hurry up! We have 15 minutes to _____ the last task.

3. The retiree said _____ to his colleagues.

4. Eric really _____ her sincere help for the project.

5. Don't _____ me too much!

2. Sentence Paraphrasing

Practice some other sentences out loud keeping the same meaning with the given sentence.

① I'm afraid I have to be on my way.

② Please stay in touch.

③ I am so flattered.

Culture Tips on Saying Goodbye

1. *Farewell Gestures:* Americans put their hand up, palm out, wrist stiff, and a back-and-forth motion with the whole forearm and hand. Europeans put their arm up and extended out, with the palm down and just the hand bobbing up and down at the wrist.

2. *Colloquial Ways of Saying "Good-bye":* People say "I'll see you later," on parting. This can be confusing since it often does not mean that the speaker expects to see you later. It is simply another way of saying "good-bye". "Take care" could be formal or casual, but is usually used with people you know or care about. You might use this in an email or written letter as well. "Have a good one" means, "have a nice day" and is used casually, but it could be used between strangers, friends, colleagues, or family members.

MAKE MY OWN DIALOGUE

Idea Bank

Think about a farewell occasion you had at your work.

Answer the following questions to talk about your unforgettable farewell memory.

1. When was it?

2. Who was the person departing? (Can be yourself or someone else)

3. Why did the farewell occasion happen?

4. What did you do to say farewell? Why is it unforgettable?

5. Do you still keep in touch? If you do, how?

Class Discussion

What kind of farewell occasions are there in business settings? If there are more ideas or students come up with other ideas, you can add them to the list.

1. Moving to another team
2. Departing to another company
3. Finishing a limited time project with a task force team

When making a farewell speech, what should you include?

1. Express appreciation to the person with whom you worked.
2. Describe your emotions for the place or position you are leaving.

    The classical three are: anticipation, excitement, and apprehension.
3. Stating a grateful tribute to the people who are remaining

---

My Own Dialogue

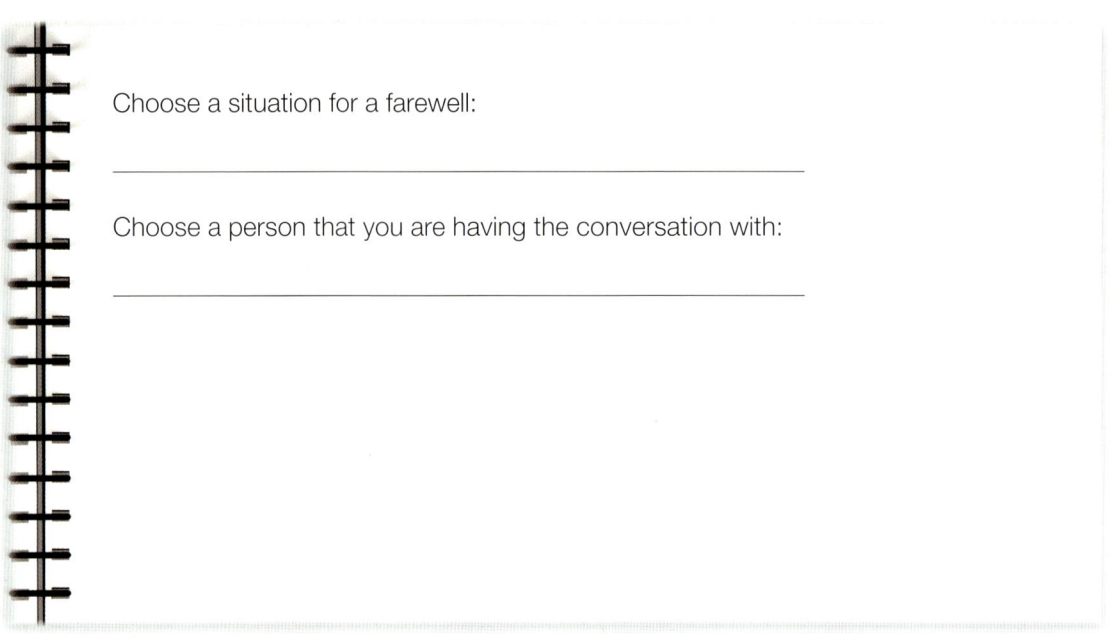

Choose a situation for a farewell:

_____

Choose a person that you are having the conversation with:

_____

 Based on the above selections, make your own dialogue.

A:

B:

A:

B:

A:

B:

Act Out

Choose a person that you are having the conversation with:

Teacher's Model Dialogue

Ms. Placid and Mr. Blanks are saying goodbye after a conference.

A: Mr. Blanks, how did you enjoy the conference?

B: I really liked the session about new marketing trends. I had read about the trends in recent articles, but the session speaker actually brought up some real cases. It helped me understand a lot better.

A: I'm glad you found it interesting. I'm really sorry, but I'd better leave now or I'll miss my flight.

B: It's been a pleasure talking with you over the conference.

A: I learned a lot from you about the market situation too. I think this business trip was very useful. I really appreciate everything you've done for me. Give me a call next time you are in New York.

B: Oh, That reminds me that I will be having a meeting in New York in two weeks. I need to discuss the schedule with my client though. I'll email you when my itinerary is confirmed.
Have a safe journey!

A: I look forward to seeing you soon. Take care! Bye!

Business English

Telephoning
& Socializing